ZERO-BASE PLANNING AND BUDGETING

Improved cost control and resource allocation

ZERO-BASE PLANNING AND BUDGETING

Improved cost control and resource allocation

Paul J. Stonich

with

John C. Kirby, Jr.

Howard P. Weil

Kent A. Thompson

Eric E. von Bauer

DOW JONES-IRWIN
Homewood, Illinois 60430

First Printing, June 1977

ISBN 0-87094-143-7
Library of Congress Catalog Card No. 77-6162
Printed in the United States of America

To our clients who helped us
develop the ideas presented in this
book; and to our families who gave
us their support.

Preface

Zero-Base Planning and Budgeting, in which each budget item is analyzed from a starting point of zero, was developed in the late 1960s as a budgeting mechanism and has since then been expanded to become a larger part of corporate planning and control systems.

This book is based on the authors' experiences designing and implementing the system in over 75 organizations. These implementations have included telephone, pharmaceutical, heavy manufacturing, consumer products, chemical and fiber, high technology, glass, moving and storage, broadcasting, paper, light manufacturing, electronics, transportation companies; banks, insurance, and service companies; and a number of governmental bodies.

Applications have been made in the United States, Canada, and Mexico and have included all functional areas of management including marketing, manufacturing overhead, engineering, research and development, and all headquarters' functions.

From the background of these experiences we provide in this book: (1) a clear description of the process; (2) summarizations and evaluations of the results achieved by organizations that have used Zero-Base Planning and Budgeting; (3) information that will aid the reader in deciding if Zero Base is appropriate for his or her organization; and (4) materials that will help interested readers design and implement Zero-Base Planning and Budgeting.

Chapter 1 defines the Zero-Base process; compares Zero Base with other budgeting systems; discusses the concept as it relates to the total planning and control process; offers criteria to answer who should use it and who should avoid it; and summarizes users' responses to a questionnaire. Chapter 2 provides a detailed explanation of how the Zero-Base Planning and Budgeting process works. Chapter 3 identifies specific functional areas of the organization in which Zero-Base Planning and Budgeting applies; and suggests design and implementation practices that are particularly well suited to those areas. Chapter 4 consists of the presentation of summaries of five cases, with a matrix that indexes various points of special interest in the cases for the reader. The complete cases, with a sixth teaching case, are included in an Appendix at the end of the book. In Chapter 5, we use the same step-by-step approach used in Chapter 2 to explain the process. The emphasis in this chapter, however, is on the problems—both psychological and mechanical, that are frequently encountered in an implementation.

Our thanks for help in preparing this book go first to our many clients who have provided the "laboratory" for the application of these new ideas. A number of our clients have helped us in preparing cases and in defining problems and developing solutions.

Many members of our firm, MAC, Inc., have contributed directly and indirectly to this book through their experiences with Zero-Base Planning and Budgeting. We wish to thank them for their contribution. Frederick W. Harvey helped prepare portions of this book and we are grateful for his assistance.

Peter A. Pyhrr, the originator of the process at Texas Instruments and a former employee of MAC, Inc., deserves special thanks for bringing the Zero Base concept to our attention in the early 1970s.

Our editor, Ellen Walvoord, sharpened our drafts and improved the text. Mary McLaughlin and Thelma Baker, office secretaries, suffered cheerfully through numerous drafts.

May 1977   **Paul J. Stonich**
                                                                    Northbrook, Illinois

Contents

Zero Base: A comparison with other budgeting processes; where it fits in the total planning system; criteria for its use

Zero-Base Budgeting, a new kid on the block in 1970, has matured with considerable grace into a respectable resident in the community of management. The Zero-Base approach, developed at Texas Instruments to meet the specific needs of volatile sales patterns and changing business mix, has demonstrated a remarkable efficacy in a wide range of applications since that first implementation.[1]

In the environment of business and government today, as when the process was developed, the ability of an organization to reallocate resources effectively to areas with the highest payoff is crucial. The flexibility to adapt to fluctuating economic conditions has also become increasingly important. The process has been applied in both good economic times and bad—the major difference between such applications is one of emphasis. In bad times, management is concerned with cost cutting; in periods of growth, with resource reallocation.

Typical budgeting efforts produce a set of numbers derived from last year's budget. Those numbers, however, neither justify the need for the activity or function to which they're assigned, nor do they identify the effectiveness or priority of that function.

Zero-Base Planning and Budgeting involves decision making from the lowest levels of management to the top. Managers are required to analyze each budget item—whether already existing or newly proposed—so that the starting point for the development of the budget is zero. As an end product, a body of structured data is obtained that enables management to allocate funds confidently to the areas of highest potential gains.

[1] Peter A. Pyhrr was a member of the team that first successfully refined the Zero-Base concept and placed it in an existing budgeting framework at Texas Instruments in 1969. The Texas Instruments implementation is fully described in Pyhrr's book: *Zero-Base Budgeting: A Practical Management Tool for Evaluating Expenses* (New York: John Wiley & Sons, Inc., 1973).

The Zero-Base approach cannot be used for the entire corporate budget. It is applicable to operations and programs over which management has some discretion. In industry, the process can be used to develop administrative and general support, marketing, research, engineering, manufacturing support, and capital budgets. It cannot be used for direct labor, direct material, and some direct overhead. These costs are usually budgeted through standard costing procedures. In government, the process can be used to develop the entire budget.

A formal definition of Zero-Base Planning and Budgeting is offered at this point: It is a comprehensive, analytically structured process that allows management to make allocation decisions about nondirect costs.

A brief explanation of the terms used in that definition follows:

Comprehensive, analytically structured. Zero-Base Planning and Budgeting establishes a consistent framework within which all managers analyze their operations in terms of objectives, alternatives, performance measurements (both qualitative and quantitative) and incremental cost/benefit. The managers are required to provide cost/benefit analyses for several increments of service and cost. The first increment is below the current level of service and cost. Additional increments of service and cost are then added as the manager completes his analysis.

Allocation decisions. Top management is able to make effective resource allocation decisions by analyzing costs and benefits of each increment within the prioritization or ranking process. Top management chooses which increments (minimum or higher) will be funded through the ranking process.

Nondirect costs. Zero-Base Planning and Budgeting is not applicable to direct costs such as labor and material. It deals with nondirect expenses such as pure overhead and other staff support activities.

ZERO BASE COMPARED WITH OTHER PLANNING AND BUDGETING SYSTEMS

The Zero-Base process pulls together a number of techniques that are already used in planning and control. These include incremental analysis, the setting of objectives or goals, alternative analysis, cost/benefit analysis, performance measurement, and line-item budgeting. Zero Base integrates these techniques within a systematic framework.

In government and industry today many different budgeting systems are used. The most prevalent one is incremental budgeting, which takes the existing budget as given and analyzes the additions or subtractions from that base. Other budgeting approaches that have some of the elements of Zero Base are Planning-Programming-Budgeting (PPB), performance budgeting, project budgeting, flexible budgeting, and certain planning analyses. The key difference between incremental budgeting and Zero-Base Budgeting is that Zero Base does not build from a base of last year's budget.[2]

[2] The previous year's budget is used, however, for comparative purposes as the final Zero-Base Budget is prepared.

Existing operations, functions, and activities are subjected to a cost/benefit analysis just as all new activities are.

Using Zero Base, management can emphasize the purpose of the unit being planned, review the necessary activities to fulfill the purpose, and finally assess the required dollars for carrying out the activities. The incremental approach is focused on the dollar expenditure—often extrapolating dollars from the previous year's costs.

With the Zero-Base process, individual managers at all levels are encouraged to think about performing their functions in different ways. Traditional incremental budgeting often does not encourage this kind of thinking. Thus, one of the major ideas of Zero-Base Planning and Budgeting is the identification of alternative methods of operation. Often the suggestion of these new methods occurs at the "grass roots" level of the organization.

The process gives general management choices rather than a hard and fast budget that can only be accepted, rejected, or changed through an arduous or arbitrary process. Figure 1-1 summarizes the differences between incremental budgeting and Zero Base.

FIGURE 1-1
Differences between incremental budgeting and Zero Base

Incremental	*Zero Base*
Starts from existing base.	Starts with "clean slate."
Examines cost/benefits for new activities.	Examines cost/benefits for all activities.
Starts with dollars.	Starts with purposes and activities.
Does not examine new ways of operating as integral part of process.	Explicitly examines new approaches.
Results in a "take it or leave it" budget.	Results in a choice of several levels of service and cost.

Typically, traditional overhead budgets are prepared at the cost center level of the organization and flow up to general management. With few indications other than dollar guidelines, top management has very little opportunity to shape the activities that will be undertaken in the organization since the budget proposals were probably prepared using the previous year as a base. Those proposals do not include a description of separate activities proposed to be undertaken by the budget unit. Rarely are there intermediate steps in the process in which top management has an opportunity to review budgets from the standpoint of activities performed.

As a result, the dollars aspect of the budget is often revised to meet the profit goals of general management, but little attention is paid to the activities aspect. Sometimes an arbitrary reduction is imposed from the top down. Zero-Base Planning and Budgeting, on the other hand, provides general management with several levels of service and cost from which to choose. Thus, once the Zero-Base Budget is prepared by the cost centers, it serves as a data base upon which the general management can make choices about the level of service and cost that is judged appropriate.

A PLANNING AND CONTROL FRAMEWORK: WHERE DOES ZERO-BASE PLANNING AND BUDGETING FIT?

The Zero-Base process, as we have introduced it, requires managers to decide which activities or functions should be performed and then to match their organizations' resources to those activities or functions. Once identified, a detailed analysis of the activity is performed by the manager closest to that activity. The analysis relies upon a well-coordinated, systematic framework consisting of the following steps.

1. The purposes and objectives of the activity (unit) are described.
2. Performance and work load measurements are developed.
3. Alternative ways of operating—including the current mode of operation—are described.
4. Each alternative is examined by cost/benefit analysis and the most appropriate (usually one or two) are chosen for further analysis.
5. A detailed incremental analysis is then performed. A minimum level of service is first developed. Then successive levels of service and cost are analyzed in terms of cost and output measures.
6. Detailed line-item costs are developed for each increment of service and cost.

Once the analysis is performed for all activities in an organization, decisions are made about alternatives that might be adopted and what level of service and cost should be provided. This process results in a prioritized ranking of all increments and a detailed budget. These steps are fully discussed in Chapters 2 and 5.

The brief summary of Zero Base given above illustrates the broad scope of the process. A review of the role of budgeting in the overall sphere of management systems is provided to give the reader a total perspective.

Planning and budgeting are interrelated in that the budget assigns dollar costs to the activities planned in the upcoming year. Prior to the budgeting process, several planning activities must be undertaken, as shown in Figure 1-2. Economic, industry, and market-share forecasts are prepared as long-range plans and goals are established. These serve as cornerstones upon which the budget is built.[3] The long-range plans and forecasts serve as input to the process of developing sales and volume budgets which, in turn, provide input to the process of developing variable cost and overhead budgets. The annual budget then, becomes the expression in financial terms of the annual plan. Results are compared to the budget and performance is evaluated.

D. E. Hussey further points out that because the annual plan has strong links with

---

[3]David E. Hussey, *Corporate Planning: Theory and Practice* (Elmsford, N.J.: Pergamon Press, Inc., 1974), pp. 28. A planning and control system model designed by Hussey and that model adapted to Zero Base appear in this chapter.

FIGURE 1-2
Planning-budgeting-control interrelationship

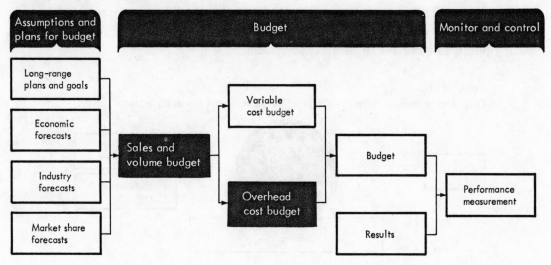

the long-range plans, the budget is also closely linked with the long-range plans. It therefore becomes more than an instrument of management control—it is a part of the implementation process of the total planning system.

Budgeting is also linked to other parts of the broad management systems in the following ways: (1) The determination of objectives. Broad objectives precede plans, which in turn, precede budgets. The plans and budgets state "how" and "how much" in more detail than the objectives. (2) Organization structure and formal communications systems help determine how the budgeting process will work.

The shaded areas in Figure 1-2 show where Zero-Base Planning and Budgeting may be used. Zero Base applies to only a part of sales and volume budgeting—all parts other than revenue and volume forecasting. Thus, components such as advertising, promotion, sales force, and sales administration are areas where Zero Base does apply.

The box representing "Overhead Cost Budget" is an area where Zero Base applies. The definition of "overhead" is broader than the normal definition, however. Overhead here includes all costs except manufacturing costs that vary directly with volume; i.e., direct labor and material. For example, Zero-Base Planning and Budgeting applies to quality control, maintenance, research, and production planning as well as the traditional overhead areas (finance, legal, administration, personnel, and others).

ZERO-BASE PLANNING AND BUDGETING AND THE TOTAL PLANNING AND CONTROL SYSTEM

Although Zero-Base Planning and Budgeting uses a number of well-known management techniques, it is not an all-encompassing planning and budgeting system. For instance, we have already noted that it does not apply to direct labor and direct material costs. In order to more readily see how Zero-Base Budgeting fits into total planning and control systems, a generalized total system will be presented.

David E. Hussey has presented a generalized planning system that provides a good starting point.[4] Figure 1-3 illustrates the system.

FIGURE 1-3
Corporate planning: Theory and practice (generalized planning system)

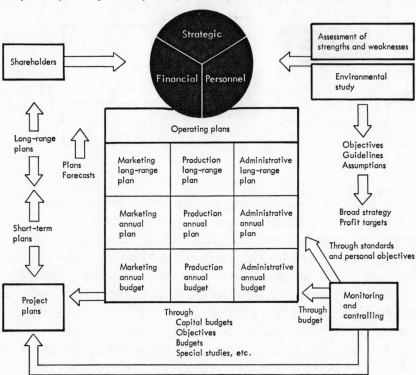

The circle and the box on which it stands illustrate a simplified view of all the plans in the system, while the other boxes and arrows show stages in the planning system.

Strategy does not arise in a vacuum, and one of the first steps in planning is to perform an appraisal of strengths and weaknesses. This is likely to lead to a number of long- and short-term decisions, including many for profit improvement. An immediate spin-off from this stage in the planning process might therefore be projects—symbolized by the box in the bottom left-hand corner.

Most companies which practice corporate planning try to achieve predetermined objectives, and the process of setting these may be considered an integral part of strategic planning. Objectives are influenced by shareholders (although usually not explicitly) and—to some degree—by the assessment of strengths and weaknesses.

The third key stage is to relate the company to its business environment. This has an

[4] Ibid., pp. 25-28.

effect on strategies through the identification of opportunities, the anticipation of threats, and the improvement of forecasts. It may help the company to see where it has to take an avoidance action. Environmental study will cover a number of factors including the economy, political events, technology, market forces, legal implications, and social factors. The study of these factors may of itself be a complex operation, and involve the application of a number of management techniques.

The chief executive, his planner, and his top management team consider the various alternatives against the background of the objectives, strengths and weaknesses, and external factors. From this, more projects may spin off (bottom left-hand corner again) for detailed planning.

From the total corporate strategy may be derived objectives and guidelines for the operating plans, and from the environmental study and its consideration in the strategic planning process may come defined planning assumptions. For a simple company, such as that shown in the diagram, the setting of objectives and targets may be easy. Most companies are much more complex, and the multi-divisional, multi-national organization may find it a very complex matter.

Long-range operating plans are properly the responsibility of those line managers in charge of the function or area concerned. The diagram shows three functional areas: in practice there may be more, or the company may be organized into subsidiaries or divisions. This additional complication does not change the principle, although it may make much harder the task of designing a planning system and introducing corporate planning.

Operating planning gives rise to plans and forecasts which flow back to the strategic planning process, where they are considered in the light of the company's objectives and strategy, and may be either accepted or returned to operating managers for refinement. In turn, the considered plans of the operating units may lead to amendments to the thinking at the strategic level and to changes in the strategic plans.

In this way there is a link between all the factors which go into the making of strategies and the thoughts of managers down the line. In many instances the managers who, as part of the top management team, work with the chief executive on strategic planning, will be the same people who initiate work on the operating plans of their particular functional areas. This is particularly so in smaller companies. In the large multi-nationals the people who complete operating plans may play little or no part in the formation of corporate strategy except for the influence their plans have on the final plans. It is possible to devise methods so that these managers have more involvement in strategic thinking, and some companies have given a great deal of attention to making this possible.

Projects may be identified at operating level and give rise to further project plans.

The company now has a completely integrated and closely co-ordinated long-range plan covering all its areas of activity. It knows what it intends to achieve, how it intends to do it, and the expected effect on financial and personal resources of these actions. Its next task is to move to implementation.

One way of doing this is through annual operating plans and the annual budget. The broad strategy and profit targets pass to the annual plans from the long-range operating plan. The annual operating plan shows the strategies and actions which have to be implemented over the forthcoming year if the plan is to be achieved. It takes these a stage further, and develops personal objectives for which named persons are responsible. If wished, this may be part of a complete system of management by objectives.

The annual budget becomes the expression in financial terms of the annual plan. Because this has strong links with the long-range plans, the budget is also closely linked with the long-range plans. It therefore becomes more than an instrument of management control in that it is a part of the implementation process of the total planning system.

Any implementation plan needs a monitoring and controlling mechanism, illustrated by the box in Figure 1-3 at the bottom right-hand corner. This mechanism ensures that the personal objectives are carried out; it checks the budget through normal methods of budgetary control and through various methods controls the performance of the projects. The outcome of measuring actual results against the plan might be a need to modify plans to some further cycle. Certainly the performance of the company is a factor which is related to its strengths and weaknesses and is then taken into account in the following year.

Zero-Base Planning and Budgeting was not included in the generalized approach provided by Hussey but it fits nicely into his scheme. Parts of five of the boxes in the diagram encompass Zero-Base Planning and Budgeting:

The box "administrative annual budget" could easily be replaced with the words

FIGURE 1-4
Hussey's model revised for Zero Base

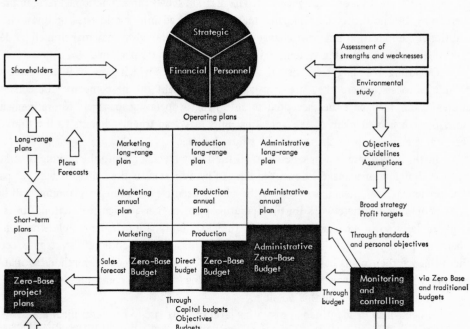

"Administrative Zero-Base Budget" because all administrative costs lend themselves to the approach and should be analyzed via Zero Base.

The "production annual budget" box should be divided into two parts. One part should deal with direct labor and material and should not involve Zero Base. Another part dealing with indirect costs, e.g., production, planning, quality control, should read "Zero Base for nondirect production costs."

The "marketing annual budget" should also be split. One part should deal with sales forecast and the other part should read "Zero Base for marketing costs."

Zero Base also is based on activities or functions. These are often in the form of projects. So the box entitled "project plans" also uses the Zero-Base technique. Finally, the Zero-Base Budget together with other budgets are used for monitoring and controlling performance. The revised diagram (Figure 1-4) shows how Zero Base fits into Hussey's generalized planning system.

ZERO BASE—WHO SHOULD USE IT?

There are no absolute formulas which, if applied, reveal a need for the process. However, from our experiences implementing the process, three categories of indications have emerged: financial, process, and managerial. As we have designed the process for individual implementations, we have attempted to discover and evaluate the need for it in this structured way. The design of the process—often overlooked by those who are attempting it for the first time—is critical to the success of the process. And the appropriate system design must be geared to the needs of the company. We can offer guidelines to help an organization determine whether or not Zero Base might be a helpful approach. But the process requires a strong commitment even when it is obvious that Zero Base is the right tool for the situation.

Financial indications

The most obvious indication of a need for a new budgeting approach is a financial one—such as the cyclicality of a business. Financial needs may be indicated by profit pressures alone; changes in business volume and mix; or costs that are not comparable among similar units in the company. It might be noted at this point that Zero Base can be effective when used in the treatment of financial crises. But, it is at least as effective in preventing financial problems. Financial indications might include:

- The organization is losing money.
- Profit margins are narrowing.
- Sales volume varies significantly from year to year or quarter to quarter.
- Business changes from year to year in such a way that support activities should be significantly altered. For instance, the mix of business may vary greatly.

Management process indications

Problems with a company's management processes may indicate a need for Zero-Base Planning and Budgeting. The critical indication in this area is the lack of ability to place priorities on different levels of service and cost. Management processes that are not working well might exhibit the following symptoms:

- Managers perceive the current budgeting system as an "exercise."
- Performance measurements are not developed or are of poor quality.
- Cost/benefit analyses are not prepared.
- The current planning and budgeting system does not consider incremental levels of cost and service.
- The current planning and budgeting system does not aid and allow management to prioritize different levels of service and cost across cost centers.

It is obvious that the roots of certain of the problems manifesting themselves in these indications should be probed. Some underlying causes may be corrected without the application of the Zero-Base process. However, a well-designed Zero-Base system together with the correction of the underlying problems may well be the most appropriate solution.

General management indications

Finally, indications at the general management level could include cost control and allocation concerns; questions about the decision-making processes; and the possibility that general management is not committed strongly to good planning. Those indications are general management's feelings that:

- Current systems do not restrain middle and lower management from unnecessary spending.
- Proper reallocation of resources between cost centers is not taking place.
- Current systems do not allow probing the organization.
- Planning, management by objective, and budgeting systems lack integration.

ZERO BASE—WHO SHOULD AVOID IT?

There are certain conditions in either an industrial or governmental situation which may preclude a successful implementation of Zero Base. Those "red flag" situations are summarized:

1. Top management is not interested in using the process and chances are low that the interest level is going to increase. Some of the attitudes expressed in response to a questionnaire sent to *Fortune's* 1,000 companies were addressed to this problem, and appear later in this chapter.[5]

2. Business is stable and management is certain that its resources are properly allocated. In this situation management is certain that it is doing things right and the environment is not a factor influencing the need for change.

3. A company or governmental unit is very small and therefore can informally

---

[5] The section "What Others Think of Zero-Base Budgeting" describes the respondents' reactions to Zero-Base Planning and Budgeting. Their concerns and their positive reactions are presented along with their answers to some structured questions.

manage its organization. The cutoff seems to come at about $1,000,000 and 75 persons of Zero-Base budgetable resources.

4. If other vast changes are currently in progress, a concomitant implementation of Zero Base should not be attempted. For example, a company that is instituting management by objectives or a new reporting system probably could not devote the attention to Zero Base that it needs for successful completion.

Zero-Base Planning and Budgeting can be a very useful process, however, for a vast number of organizations. If the Zero-Base process is carefully implemented, the results can be impressive. Budget reductions of 20 percent or more have been accomplished without materially diminishing quality or function. Another strong characteristic of the process has been its adaptability as a device for resource reallocation.[6]

In other implementations, alternative methods of operation have been developed that include organizational changes, procedural changes, make/buy trade-offs and man/machine trade-offs. Some of the most important results—although difficult to quantify—have been in the areas of intraorganizational communication and effective understanding of the organization's structure. All facets of these results will be expanded in other chapters.

WHAT OTHERS THINK OF ZERO-BASE PLANNING AND BUDGETING

To gather what information we could about who is using Zero-Base Budgeting now and how they feel about it, a questionnaire was sent to *Fortune's* 1,000 companies. Responses were received from 113 of those companies; 54 indicated they had used it; 59 had not. It is probably safe to assume that the vast majority of nonrespondents had never used Zero-Base Planning and Budgeting.

Admittedly the sample is small. And the responses may be biased in favor of Zero Base because pioneers of a new process sometimes feel a need to justify their actions. The results, however, provide some indication of the users' response to the Zero-Base process.

The questionnaire was designed to test a series of assumptions by tabulating the users' ratings of several Zero-Base features. Users were also encouraged to add their candid opinions about the process in a special section.

This report on the survey first provides a forum for the comments made by users of the process; and then answers to the questionnaire are presented.

COMMENTS FROM USERS

About half of the executives responding to the questionnaire augmented their answers with comments, criticisms, and suggestions regarding Zero-Base Planning and

[6] Using MAC, Inc.'s clients as a base for reference, 36 percent of all decision units (the separate grouping of activities around which the analysis is centered) have had cost reductions of at least 5 percent. About 33 percent have had expenditure increases of at least 5 percent. In other words, the process allowed management to shift funds from one area to another to maximize effectiveness.

Budgeting. Those responses, which provide a valuable perspective, are presented in two groupings: concerns about the process and advantages of the approach.

Concerns about the process

The concerns expressed by the respondents are presented in their own words. However, they have been categorized according to the areas into which they fell:

Top management commitment vital

- "To be successful requires attentive, interested management. This may not be assumed."
- "It must be stressed again that any benefits derived from utilizing Zero-Base Planning and Budgeting will come only if management accepts the responsibility placed on them by it. They must be willing to spend the necessary time to provide guidelines and direction for the effective preparation of decision units and more importantly, time to analyze, question, evaluate, and effectively rank the decision units resulting from the process."

Process is time consuming

- "The process becomes much too cumbersome as it goes up the ladder in management. Forms need to be developed to communicate upward after they leave the first ranking manager. Also, it seems apparent to me that the second cycle of Zero Base should or could be simplified by use of abbreviated forms without losing the thrust. Somehow the process must cut down on the paper work."
- "In combination with our other management systems, it has worked very well. Some reduction in paper volume through improved forms design would reduce the work load for those who coordinate the system."
- "Some managers felt they did not have sufficient time to do the required analysis."
- "Don't get 'stuck' because of issues relating to accounting problems. Be satisfied with completing the process and identifying (not necessarily resolving) all such issues."

Cost cutting feature shouldn't be overplayed

- "When first presented, it seemed that top management viewed it solely as a budget cutting tool. It was then used specifically for that purpose. Constant attention should be directed toward developing decisions from a sounder base than that, even though Zero-Base Planning always seems to be implemented when it's necessary to cut back."
- "Had to identify a minimum level of operation even though it may not be realistic; i.e., some groups had already cut their '76 budget, but were asked to complete a decision unit at 80 percent of this."
- "Important to 'sell' as a tool for better management versus a method to cut costs."

Effective staff work needed

- "Low-profile, effective staff work is critical to make Zero-Base Budgeting effective."
- "Process seemingly not clearly spelled out; i.e., manager felt he had done what was requested only to be asked to change it again."
- "It is doubtful that the process will be self-perpetuating without constant supervision. Much of

the success of the process has to be attributed to (staff members) who had to cope with the numerous practical problems associated with the process."

Process is no panacea
- "Not a panacea for all previous budgeting/planning ills."
- "Top management should be made aware of limitations and not expect too much."
- "Zero-Base Budgeting will not and cannot replace the management process."

Process must be carefully planned and developed
- "Need a well-organized approach (plan) to implement it in an organization, absolutely."
- "We stress concept is not new, merely 'formalization' of the thought process."
- "In the area of organization planning, other techniques are needed to evaluate the organizational issues which are identified by Zero-Base Budgeting."

Advantages of the approach

Users were also helpful in describing the advantages of the process. These have been categorized, but again are presented in the words of the users.

Cost cutting
- "Provide knowledge of where and what the minimum service level is in each decision unit."
- "Recommend Zero Base as a means to cut overhead costs."
- "I feel that Zero-Base Budgeting is a good process for changing and reallocating budget levels."

Reallocating resources
- "An advantage is forced ranking of priorities."
- "A systematic way to evaluate operations and programs and to set priorities on spending levels."

Contingency planning
- "We are playing up the 'planning' aspects and getting reception to the 'contingency plan' applications of the process."
- "Provides management with added flexibility during the year in making intelligent adjustments when needed by giving added insight into the consequences and benefits involved in proposed adjustments to spending levels."
- "Provides a definitive 'blueprint' to increase or decrease activity without the necessity of doing a new plan. Since changes of this type normally generate a great deal of stress, management has a plan to follow that was carefully constructed at a time when alternatives (and increments) were logically and not emotionally determined."

Alternative methods of operation
- "Excellent tool to evaluate alternatives."

Learning about the organization
- "The main value of the system for us is in its contribution to our understanding of how the organization works, or should work."

- "Zero-Base operational planning is a high-quality substitute for the near-term planning we had been doing, and has the advantage that it seems to fit manager's needs (and the 'culture' of our organization) much better."
- "Appears to have great potential for providing data and basis for in-depth assessment of inter-functional relationships, problems, and opportunities for improvement."

Stimulating thought

- "Stimulates the thinking of subordinates and helps gather good ideas from below."
- "Clarifies the unit's role in the organization and the appropriate measures of evaluating performance."
- "The major advantage is created in reviewing each task for its relevancy and the opportunity to question alternative methods and systems."

Communication

- "Facilitates the identification of common problems or opportunities between departments."
- "Communicates problems and opportunities to higher management in addition to the 'numbers' and shifts the focus to important management concerns."
- "A good communication tool between the boss and subordinate."

QUESTIONNAIRE RESPONSES

The questionnaire (Figure 1-5) was basically designed to obtain structured answers to specific areas of inquiry. The various features of Zero Base Planning and Budgeting were presented to the users and a rating of excellent, good, fair, poor, or not applicable was requested. Cost reduction results achieved by users were also probed.

Cost cutting

Two questions (not contiguous) dealt with the use of Zero-Base Planning and Budgeting as a cost cutting tool. Respondents rated the process as follows:

1. Rate the Zero-Base Planning and Budgeting process as a process to change the total budget level.

28%	. . . .	Excellent
46%	. . . .	Good
20%	. . . .	Fair
None	. . . .	Poor
6%	. . . .	Not applicable

13. By how much was your total budget affected after implementing Zero-Base Planning and Budgeting?

12%	Decreased budget	10% or more
30%	Decreased budget	5-10%
51%	Changed budget	Less than 5%
7%	Increased budget	5% or more

It is important to note that these budget reductions were stated in dollars before the effect of inflation. Thus a 5 percent reduction during a year in which inflation was 8 percent would be equal to a 13 percent reduction in real terms. Respondents, then, perceived the process as effective in changing budget levels and actually achieved effective changes in the overall budget levels.

Reallocation

Another key feature of Zero Base is its use as a tool to reallocate resources. Users rated this feature in the following manner:

2.   Rate the Zero-Base Budgeting process as a process to reallocate costs and manpower.

34% . . . . Excellent
42% . . . . Good
20% . . . . Fair
2% . . . . Poor
2% . . . . Not applicable

General applicability

Three other questions dealt with the general applicability of the process. An evaluation of answers to the first two questions indicated that the process was perceived as useful. Answers to the third question in this category revealed users' feelings about implementing the process in the future.

11.   In general, how would you rate Zero-Base Planning and Budgeting as a management planning and control system?

28% . . . . Excellent
59% . . . . Good
13% . . . . Fair
None . . . . Poor

12.   In general, how would you compare Zero-Base Planning and Budgeting with other formal management systems?

67% . . . . Better
33% . . . . About the same
None . . . . Worse

14.   In the future how do you plan to use the Zero-Base Planning and Budgeting process?

None . . . . .   Do not plan to use process again.
43% . . . . .   Plan to use it to supplement the traditional budgeting process.
25% . . . . .   Plan to use it to replace the traditional process.
32% . . . . .   Plan to use for particular departments only.

Intangible features

Finally, we wanted to sample user response to a whole series of other less tangible features. The following table indicates users' views of those features.

Rate Zero-Base Planning and Budgeting as a process to:	Percentage				
	Excellent	Good	Fair	Poor	Not applicable
Learn more about the organization	55%	42%	3%	—	—
Manage overhead activities with flexibility	20	54	23	3%	—
Improve efficiency and effectiveness within the organization . . .	18	58	18	3	3%
Improve communications across the organization	16	47	29	3	5
Develop alternative methods of operation	15	46	36	3	—
Plan organizational changes	13	39	24	16	8
Identify organizational issues that are not directly within the scope of Zero-Base Budgeting	10	29	42	16	3

FIGURE 1-5
Total—All responses to Zero-Base Planning and Budgeting Questionnaire

Excel-lent	Good	Fair	Poor	Not appli-cable	(Respondents were asked to rate the Zero-Base Planning and Budgeting process by placing an "X" on the appropriate line beside each phrase.)
28%	46%	20%	—	6%	1. As a process to change the total budget level.
34	42	20	2%	2	2. As a process to reallocate costs and manpower.
15	46	36	3	—	3. As a process to develop alternative methods of operation.
55	42	3	—	—	4. As a process to learn more about the organization.
16	47	29	3	5	5. As a process to improve communications across the organization.
10	29	42	16	3	6. As a process to identify organizational issues that are not directly within the scope of Zero-Base Planning and Budgeting.
13	35	35	11	5	7. As a process to evaluate staff performance.
13	39	24	16	8	8. As a process to plan organizational changes.
18	58	18	3	3	9. As a process to improve efficiency and effectiveness within the organization.
20	54	23	3	—	10. As a process to manage overhead activities with flexibility.
28	59	13	—	—	11. In general, how would you rate Zero-Base Planning and Budgeting as a management planning and control system?

12. In general, how would you compare Zero-Base Planning and Budgeting with other formal management systems?

67% Better

— Worse

33% About the same

— Not applicable

13. By how much was your total budget affected after implementing Zero-Base Planning and Budgeting?

12% Decreased more than 10%.

30% Decreased between 5%-10%.

51% Less than a 5% change.

3% Increased between 5%-10%.

3% Increased more than 10%.

14. In the future, how do you plan to use the Zero-Base Planning and Budgeting process?

43% As a supplement to the traditional budgeting process.

25% As a replacement for the traditional budgeting process.

32% As a planning process for particular departments only.

— Do not plan to use the process.

15. Any comments, criticisms, and suggestions you have concerning Zero-Base Planning and Budgeting would be appreciated.

2

The Zero-Base process
step by step

The Zero-Base concept is fashionable today. It is being suggested on many fronts as a miracle process that can dramatically and mystically transform an organization overnight. That, of course, isn't the case.

It is a good and useful management tool that is applicable to operations and programs over which management has some discretion. But the successful implementation of Zero Base is a difficult and involved process. It requires commitment, understanding, and hard work from all levels of management.

THE ZERO-BASE PLANNING AND BUDGETING PROCESS

The Zero-Base Planning and Budgeting process is explained here in a six-step framework. It is only reasonable to add a caveat that the six-step process presented is a generalization for the convenience of the reader. Specific applications should draw on the general approach, but must be tailor-designed to meet an organization's individual needs with consideration given to: (a) environmental factors; (b) the "culture" of the organization; and (c) the objectives of the organization. Each of these points is explored further in the following chapters.

The process of implementing Zero Base requires the involvement of managers at all levels in the organization. The interaction of managers is unavoidable—by design—as the various steps in the process are carried out. Specific problems arising in each step are illustrated in Chapter 5; applications of the step in different functional areas are given in Chapter 3. The process is both top-down and bottom-up. Figure 2-1 illustrates the iterative nature of the process. The horizontal axis shows the six steps; the vertical axis shows management involvement.

FIGURE 2-1
Management involvement in the Zero-Base process

Management involvement	Process step					
	1 Develop planning assumptions	2 Identify decision units	3 Analyze decision units	4 Review and reallocate resources	5 Prepare budget	6 Evaluate performance
Top management	X			X		X
Planning and controllers department				X	X	X
Ranking manager		X		X		X
Decision unit manager		X	X			X

Step 1. Develop planning assumptions

The Zero-Base process begins with the development of planning assumptions for the upcoming year. The assumptions serve as an input to the various operating departments for their individual budget preparation efforts. To analyze the operation effectively, the lower level manager requires planning assumptions about inflation rates and salary increases the same as a manager preparing a traditional budget. In addition to these economic and planning assumptions, the lower level manager requires information about service-level requirements for allied departments. The more complete the assumptions and plans, the easier it is for the manager to prepare his budget.

Step 2. Identify "decision units"

The next step is the identification of the "decision units." The decision unit is the separate grouping of activities around which analysis is centered. The decision unit can be the traditional cost center or budget unit or it can encompass a group of activities. Decision units may also include: special projects or programs; activities that apply across the organization such as marketing or training; objects of expense; or services rendered. Figure 2-2 lists some sample decision units.

Decision units are literally named—units of activities that can be analyzed for discretionary decisions. Thus, fixed activities limited by laws, industry practice, or other constraints are separated from those activities where action can be effected. Involuntary expenditures that are part of an operating budget are also often excluded.

Decision units need to be established at an organizational level high enough so that the person responsible for the operation of the unit (the decision unit manager) has effective control over the budget dollars. The advantage to both top management and the decision unit manager is that his or her plan is presented not only in terms of dollars to be spent, but also of the activities to be performed.

It is desirable for decision units to be roughly similar in size in terms of both personnel and dollars. Proper analysis cannot be performed on very large decision units because they tend to include a multiplicity of activities, thus complicating the incremental analysis which takes place later.

FIGURE 2-2
Sample decision units

Department or area	Decision unit
Engineering	Standards and design
	Drafting
	Maintenance
Plant	Customer service
Business research and planning	Customer requirement tests
Finance	Project '77
	Treasury
	Payable
Organizational	Management development
Development	Services
Marketing	Advertising
	Direct sales
Companywide	Training
	Travel and entertainment
Administration	EDP project

A unit that is too small is not easily analyzed either, because it is difficult to develop practical lower or higher levels of service. Also, if units are very small, the result is a larger number of them which causes the total analysis to be unwieldy.

Typical decision units include between 5 and 15 people and a dollar budget of about $150,000 to $400,000 on a full-cost basis. However, certain decision units with large clerical staffs performing one routine function could possibly include 50 or more people. A few decision units may be smaller or larger than the range expressed. These rules of thumb seem to apply to all organizations regardless of industry or size of organization. Further discussion of identification of decision units may be found in all following chapters.

Step 3. Analyze each decision unit

Zero-Base Planning and Budgeting is designed to involve all levels of management in the analysis. Analysis at the decision unit level is the heart of the process. It is the most time consuming and the area of most vulnerability. If insufficient or inaccurate data is developed, it will affect the entire planning and budgeting process.

Decision unit objectives

A decision unit manager begins the analysis by specifying his objective and the purpose of the decision unit. Several examples are in Figure 2-3.

Description of current operation

Following the writing of his objectives, the decision unit manager describes how he currently operates and the resources he utilizes—both people and dollars. Obviously, if a decision unit manager sets out to describe his operation in great detail, this could be a very time-consuming exercise. Referencing ordinary office equipment such as

FIGURE 2-3
Examples of decision unit objectives

Production control

To plan, organize, direct, coordinate, and control the orderly flow of turbine components through the manufacturing processes of fabrication, machine, assembly, and shipment; the goal being delivery of a complete product, on time, in accordance with shop schedules, financial planning, and customer requirements.

Marketing administration

To manage the product sales and marketing support functions with responsibility for preparation and administration of pricing, proposals, contracts, sales presentation materials, training programs, litigation administration, and special projects.

Internal audit

To assist management in evaluating and recommending appropriate policies and procedures to ensure the safeguard of assets, the reliability of the financial system, the adequacy of the internal controls and the performance of the operating units in accordance with management's overall profit objectives.

Materials engineering and technology

To provide metallurgical services to manufacturing, purchasing, service engineering, generations systems engineering, and development engineering on materials and processes used in company products.

These objectives are considerably more general than those found in Management by Objective systems. However, the specificity of objectives is expanded later in the analysis when performance measurements are developed.

desks, pencils, and paper clips is definitely not the intention of this step in the process. Rather, the description should set out those elements of resources which are unique to the operation—in addition to the numbers and types of employees that contribute their efforts to the decision unit. Operations should, wherever possible, be described in order of the flow of work. An example of a typical description for a manufacturing support group follows:

> First, we provide factory support by resolving the error appraisal notices, and then we coordinate and follow the repair and replacement of existing components returned for repair. Form clerks process the service order forms we receive from Department 421 and make up the service work schedule.

Other samples of these descriptions appear in Chapter 3.

Work load and performance measurements

Work load and performance measurements are next developed to examine the strengths and weaknesses of the manager's current approach and to describe his objective in greater detail.

Some sample performance measurements related to the earlier objective example might include:

- Production control—on-time delivery performance.
- Regional sales managers—number of customer requests for cancellations and/or reschedules.
- Internal audit—cycle for audit coverage of reporting units.
- Materials engineering and technology—number of failure analyses performed.

Other examples of work load and performance measurements appear in Chapter 3. A more detailed explanation of establishing those measurements is found in Chapter 5.

Alternatives

The manager next considers alternative ways of operating. Examples of different operational modes are: (1) centralizing the functions; (2) decentralizing the functions; (3) contracting for the function; (4) combining the function with other activities; or (5) eliminating the function. After reviewing both the current method of operation as well as new approaches, the manager, in consultation with his superior, chooses the best method of operation on the basis of an analysis showing the advantages and disadvantages of each alternative, as evaluated by performance measurements.

The proposing of alternatives is a departure from "normal" thinking which usually focuses not on finding different ways to do the job, but on finding ways to improve the current process. Imagination is called for in responding to this part of the process, and decision unit managers are encouraged to make a real effort to support the new alternative with an estimate of what benefits and risks might be associated with it.

Incremental analysis

After the appropriate alternative is selected, the incremental analysis begins. The decision unit manager determines which is the most important service need provided by his unit.

The highest priority needs comprise the first or minimum increment of service. In theory the minimum increment is determined by selecting the amount of service that the organization must absolutely undertake—the amount below which it would be impossible to provide any meaningful service. The minimum is often specified not to exceed a certain percentage below the current level.

The practical problem of getting managers to submit reasonable minimums is solved by specifying a so-called maximum minimum below current.

Thus, the first increment offers a narrower range of services than is presently provided or reduced quality or quantity of service. By identifying a minimum service level, the manager is forced to focus on the functions his unit provides. Establishment of the minimum increment is treated extensively in Chapter 5.

Several increments may be required before the cumulative total approximates or

FIGURE 2-4
Increments for purchasing department

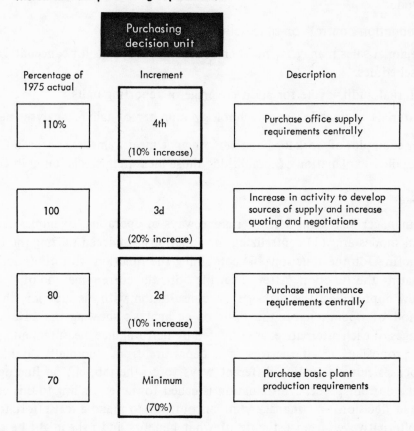

exceeds current service levels. Additional increments of service and cost are developed with each successive increment containing those services which are next in order of priority. Increment number two consists of the second-priority services or functions. This process continues until all the functions of the decision unit are identified. Figures 2-4 and 2-5 show possible increments for a purchasing department and a mail delivery department.

Work load and performance measurements are included in each analysis since they identify meaningful quantitative measurements that assist in evaluating the effectiveness and efficiency of each increment. Such measurements may include divisions served, number of work units or tasks performed, cost effectiveness, or unit cost. They may reflect incremental performance at each level or they may reflect the cumulative effect of adding each increment.

Examples of the summary data prepared by decision unit managers in charge of corporate sales and quality control are presented in Figures 2-6 and 2-7. The examples show, in summarized fashion, all the analysis performed by the decision unit managers.

The analysis includes:

1. The objective of the decision unit.
2. The current method of operations and required resources.

FIGURE 2-5
Increments for mail delivery department

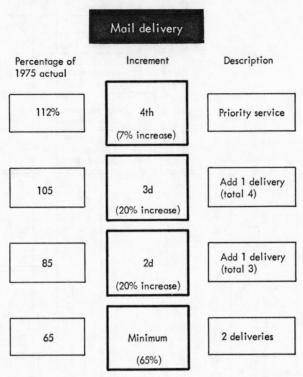

3. The alternatives considered and the reasons for rejecting whatever was not used.
4. The minimum increment of service, its cost and its benefit in terms of work load and performance. Additional increments of service, cost, and associate benefits.

Step 4. Review and reallocate resources—the ranking

The increments developed by decision unit managers provide top-level managers with the basic information for critical resource allocation. The heart of this process is the prioritization or ranking. The first prioritization actually occurs at the decision unit level when the manager recommends funding of a particular function prior to funding of another function. In many cases, however, the decision unit manager merely identifies increasing levels of the same service as part of his analysis.

The next ranking occurs at the level immediately above the decision unit manager. This ranking takes place when the manager meets with all of his decision unit managers to prioritize the increments—based on the objectives of the group and the organization. This results in a ranking table similar to the one shown in Figure 2-8.

The ranking is based on the written analyses and discussions between the decision unit managers and the ranking manager. The written costs and benefits of each increment are the formal criteria for the ranking; however, the give and take of the meetings

FIGURE 2-6. Decision unit summary

DECISION UNIT NAME:
Corporate Sales

1. OBJECTIVE OF DECISION UNIT:

    To manage all domestic sales so that present customers receive satisfactory service, gross revenues increase by 12 percent, new customer sales increase by 20 percent, and contribution margin of salesstaff be at least double the cost of salesstaff.

2. CURRENT OPERATIONS AND REQUIRED RESOURCES:

    There is a sales manager, nine salaried salespeople, two warehouseworkers, one office clerk, and one secretary. Each salesperson is assigned an exclusive territory in the Northeast and Eastern United States.

3. LIST ALTERNATIVE WAYS WHICH COULD ACCOMPLISH OBJECTIVE AND REASON FOR NOT USING IN 1977:

    a. Use commissioned sales representatives — technical nature of product requires services of an exclusive salesperson.

4. SUMMARY OF INCREMENTS FOR 1977 SERVICE PROVIDED (Identify the "current" level):

| SUMMARY OF INCREMENTS FOR 1977 SERVICE PROVIDED | Increment number | Incremental | | Cumulative | | | | Work-load/Performance summary | | | | |
| | | | | | | | | Quality | | Quantity | | |
		Expense	Employees	Expense	%(b)	Employees	%(b)	Customer service complaints (per month)	Delay in order processing (days)	Gross sales revenue ($000)	New customer sales ($000)	Contribution margin ($000) (cum.)
Employ Sales Manager, 7 Salespeople, 2 Warehouseworkers, 1 Secretary	1 of 4	280,000	11	280,000	95	11	79	9	8	4,000	600	700
Add 2 salespeople	2 of 4	66,500	2	346,500	117	13	93	7	10	5,000	1,100	840
Add 1 office clerk	3 of 4	10,200	1	356,700	121	14	100	5	3	5,000	1,100	840
Add 1 salesperson	4 of 4	31,000	1	387,700	131	15	107	3	3	5,400	1,400	880
	of											
	of											
1976 Forecast expense and employees				295,100		14		5	3	4,400	900	750

Zero Base planning and budgeting

FIGURE 2-7. Decision unit summary

DECISION UNIT NAME:
Quality Control

1. OBJECTIVE OF DECISION UNIT:

To insure that manufactured product is made under conditions that provide maximum quality, yield, and production rate; and to monitor the quality of all packaged products to insure that established quality standards are met.

2. CURRENT OPERATIONS AND REQUIRED RESOURCES:

There are four inspectors who analyze and grade product samples. Inspection occurs at 3,000-pound intervals, on a continuous production cycle (24 hours per day—7 days per week). There is one laboratory foreman who directly supervises inspectors and investigates customer complaints. There is one general foreman who performs special analyses and maintains department records. There is one department supervisor who has responsibility for all phases of quality control administration.

3. LIST ALTERNATIVE WAYS WHICH COULD ACCOMPLISH OBJECTIVE AND REASON FOR NOT USING IN 1977:

a. Inspect more or less often than every 3,000 pounds—experience has shown that the present interval is optimal from both a cost and a quality perspective.
b. Have the R&D department perform special projects such as a yield study—would have to be delegated by plant manager.

4. SUMMARY OF INCREMENTS FOR 1977 SERVICE PROVIDED (Identify the "current" level):

	Increment number	Incremental Expense	Incremental Employees	Cumulative Expense	Cumulative %(b)	Cumulative Employees	Cumulative %(b)	Work-load/Performance summary Quality: Number of customer complaints per month	Quality: Percentage rejected	Quantity: Number of special analyses per month	Quantity: Production rate improvement (%) (cum.)
Employ department supervisor and 4 inspectors	1 of 4	77,500	5	77,500	75	5	71	10	5		
Add laboratory foreman	2 of 4	14,200	1	91,700	89	6	86	6	3.5	-	
Add general foreman (current)	3 of 4	13,800	1	105,500	102	7	100	3	2.5	2	
Add chemist for process improvement	4 of 4	17,500	1	123,000	119	8	114	3	1.5	2	10
	of										
	of										
1976 Forecast expense and employees				103,400		7		3	2.5	2	

FIGURE 2-8
Sample ranking table

(1) Organizational units being ranked		(2) Prepared by	(3) Date	(4) Page
Marketing		B. Collins	6/9/76	1 of 1

(5) Decision unit increments		(6) 1977 proposed	(7) 1977 cumulative	(8) 1976 forecast	(9) Percent change 1977 ÷ 1976 × 100
Rank	Increment number	Expense	Expense	Expense	Expense
1. Corporate sales	1 of 4	280,000	280,000	295,100	60
2. Advertising	1 of 3	85,000	365,000	104,000	78
3. Marketing administration	1 of 3	62,100	427,100	71,100	91
4. Corporate sales	2 of 4	66,500	493,600		105
5. Advertising	2 of 3	24,600	518,200		110
6. Corporate sales	3 of 4	10,200	528,400		112
7. Marketing administration	2 of 3	13,400	541,800		115
8. Advertising	3 of 3	17,600	559,400		119
9. Corporate sales	4 of 4	31,000	590,400		126
10. Marketing administration	3 of 3	12,500	602,900		128
	of				
	of				
	of				
	of				
	of				
Total		602,900	602,900	470,200	128

are also vital in determining the priorities. Further discussions of this phase appear in several cases, as indexed in Chapter 3, and in Chapters 4 and 5.

Figure 2-8 shows the prioritization of the increments, their costs, cumulative expenses, and a comparison with the previous year's budget. For instance, the first increment of corporate sales was given the highest priority. It was followed by the first increment of advertising at a cost of $85,000. The second increment of marketing administration is ranked seventh, behind the third increment of corporate sales and the second increment of advertising. This illustrates how the process works to reallocate resources. If management decided to fund only through the increment ranked number six, corporate sales would receive a total of $356,700, an increase of 21 percent over last year's $295,000 budget. Marketing administration would receive only $62,100—or 87 percent of last year's budget of $71,100.

The process of ranking usually involves group meetings to develop the appropriate priorities. (A full discussion of those ranking meetings appears in the Chapter 4 cases and in Chapter 5.)

A useful mechanism is a matrix like the one in Figure 2-9. Each increment's costs are listed and the benefits are discussed. After each increment is reviewed and funded for a decision unit, the next one is put "in competition" with the other increments. For instance, once approvals are given to all increments to the left of the heavy line in the figure, the fourth increment of corporate sales competes with the third of advertising and the second of marketing administration.

FIGURE 2-9
Decision unit—increment matrix

INCREMENT

DECISION UNIT	1	2	3	4	5
Corporate sales	$280,000	$66,500	$10,200	$31,000	
Advertising	$ 85,000	$24,600	$17,600		
Marketing administration	$ 62,100	$13,400	$12,500		

At the next ranking level, the process becomes more complex. This ranking manager works from the ranking tables already developed and the backup analysis.

It is obvious that establishing ranking priorities at the next level and above could become overwhelming if not handled properly. To assist in the process and to eliminate a flood of unnecessary paper, several procedures are followed. A file of one-page summary sheets for each decision unit is maintained and used if specific questions occur. The "gray area" of the ranking tables is the major focus for decision making.[3]

Often separate analyses summarizing key issues are prepared by staff. The emphasis is upon identifying organizations as having high, medium, or low potential

[3] The manager draws the line on the basis of his proposed request for funding in the upcoming year. He bases his request upon the cost/benefits of the increments under him and upon his perception of the "reasonableness" of his request. Obviously, if the request is way out of line, the ranking manager will draw a new line and review the "gray area" above and below the new line. In the extreme case, the ranking manager may be forced to review all increments. This rarely occurs, being caused by either incompetent managers or ones who are attempting to subvert the system. This problem is discussed in Chapter 5.

for cost reduction and recommending a funding range for each ranked organization. Once the funding lines have been drawn, the final product of these meetings and analyses is a ranking table for the entire organization which indicates the increments that have been approved, those that have not been funded, and the costs of each approved and disapproved increment. The ranking table is a record of all the decisions that have been made in the Zero-Base Planning and Budgeting process. Not only does it show what will and will not be funded in the upcoming year, it also ranks activities in priority so that adjustments during the year can be made more easily.

It is important to note that the ranking process serves two distinct purposes. The obvious purpose is to make resource allocation choices. The second purpose is less tangible, but equally important. The ranking process provides a forum for communication. Good ranking meetings result in all participants learning together about the organization and its needs.

Step 5. Prepare detailed budgets

When the allocation decisions have been made, detailed budgets are prepared. The ranking table drawn up by management; and the individual decision unit forms which show all increments provide the basis for this mechanical function.

Figure 2-10 illustrates the final budget with the approved priorities. This budget, although prepared in a vastly different fashion than traditional budgets, is similar in format to the end product of the traditional approach. The cost breakdowns (e.g., salaries, bonuses, travel), feed directly into the company's existing budgeting and control system.

Step 6. Evaluate performance

Zero-Base Planning and Budgeting provides two types of data for management review: financial data as well as work load and performance measurements that can be monitored periodically. Decision unit managers can be held responsible for costs and performance. To be effective, Zero-Base Planning and Budgeting needs to be reinforced through measurement and control. There are several methods of evaluation:

- Monthly financial review of each decision unit and ranking unit. This is a traditional financial review based on budget compared to actual. It is based solely on costs expended.

- Quarterly output review of each decision unit and ranking unit. This review of the planned output with the organization is the key to the successful use of the system. The performance measurements are used to make this evaluation.

- Quarterly (or as needed) plan and budget revisions for the company and decision units. A process whereby orderly revisions to plans can be made is essential. This is based on (a) performance to date, and (b) environmental factors facing the company such as profit pressures.

FIGURE 2-10

Sample summary budget for quality control decision unit

(1) DECISION UNIT NAME Production Planning		(2) ORGANIZATION Sales Service			(3) PREPARED BY W. J. Ireton			(4) DATE 8/29/76	
Account codes	Description	1976 Forecast	1977 Proposed increments						1977 Total of all increments	1977 Approved plan
			1 of 1	2 of 2	3 of 3	4 of 4			
001	Salaries and related	98,400	66,500	13,800	15,950	14,850			111,?00	
005	Supplies and exp.	150	175	10	15	45			245	
006	Postage	110	100	10	15	15			140	
007	Telephone and teleg.	6,000	4,000	1,200	500	400			6,100	
008	Travel and entertainment	3,750	2,500	1,500	500	500			5,000	
012	Purchased services	1,275	1,000	250	100	400			1,750	
014	Automobile expense	4,700	3,500	1,500	575	200			5,775	
019	Air fares	4,200	3,200	1,350	450	225			5,225	
306	Supplies – data processing	3,000	2,500	225	100	475			3,300	
	Total controllable	121,585	83,475	19,845	18,205	17,110			138,635	
	Allocations									

Summary

Figure 2-11 summarizes in simple terms how the Zero-Base Planning and Budgeting process works. Suppose that an organization has three functions: (1) quality control, (2) production planning, and (3) maintenance and protection. The first step is to identify the functions or activities. Then each activity is analyzed. Finally, alternatives are chosen and increments are prepared.

In the figure, each of the four increments represents groups of services that can be provided with various amounts of resources. The increments start below the current budget level (represented by the broken line) and end above the current level.

Once the analysis is complete, each increment is evaluated via its costs and

FIGURE 2-11
Graphical representation of decision unit increment structure

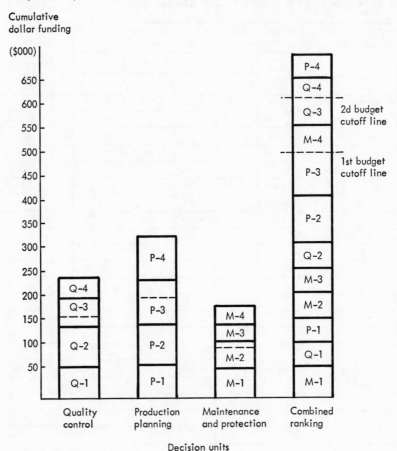

Decision units

benefits and a prioritization between the competing increments is established.

The ranking process performed by the department manager results in prioritizing the 12 increments identified previously (three decision units times four increments each). This process allocates resources to the highest priority areas first. The figure shows that the first three increments ranked were M-1, Q-1, and P-1. However, M-2 and M-3 took priority over P-2 and Q-2, thus indicating that funding up through the third increment of the maintenance and protection function took precedence over the second level of either the production planning or quality control functions.

Thus, should the available funds be only at the "first cutoff line," then all increments through P-3 would be budgeted. Should the budget be higher ("second cutoff line"), additional service levels would be funded in their order of priority.

The decisions made in the ranking are then translated into budgets which are used to monitor performance.

Functional applications of Zero Base

3

Application of the Zero-Base Planning and Budgeting process may differ from department to department within the same overall implementation. As a result of our experiences with the process, we are able to categorize applications into three types: (1) pure overhead facets of business that are removed from production (e.g., accounting, personnel, head office operations); (2) those dealing with operations close to production that may vary somewhat with production (e.g., engineering, manufacturing); (3) those aspects of business that influence volume (e.g., sales/marketing).

In this chapter, four examples of applications of Zero Base to specific functional areas of an organization are discussed: (1) accounting, (2) manufacturing, (3) engineering, and (4) marketing. The differences in these applications arise principally in designing and implementing the process to complement existing characteristics or operations of each department and its staff. An exhibit provides detailed examples of objectives and performance measurements.

ACCOUNTING DEPARTMENT

Zero-Base Planning and Budgeting has proven to be a very effective process for analyzing an Accounting Department because all the operations are overhead oriented.

Decision units

Identification of appropriate decision units in accounting is less complex than in some other applications because an Accounting Department is function or activity related—in contrast to an Engineering Department, which is often project related.

The number of decision units in accounting can vary greatly—depending mainly on the size of the department. A large Accounting Department, for example, might be broken into the following decision units:

General accounting	Accounts payable	Costs and budgets
Cash and asset management	EDP	Insurance
Accounts receivable	Internal audit	Taxes

A smaller department would have fewer decision units. For example, General Accounting can cover several decision units, if their sizes are small enough to warrant such consolidation.

Statements of objectives

Once decision units are identified, a clear statement of objective for each unit must be prepared. The decision unit manager will find this statement useful for preparing his incremental analyses, while higher management levels will use the statement for reviewing these analyses.

Without clear direction as to what a decision unit is meant to accomplish, the incremental analyses will lack focus and consequently fail to meet organizational goals. The statement of objective is designed to avoid such problems.

The importance of a clear statement of objective can be illustrated by consideration of a decision unit such as General Accounting. What activities does General Accounting typically include? Does it include the accounts payable function, or is this function analyzed separately? What is the purpose of even having this decision unit? Following are several decision unit objective statements for accounting activities.

Internal audit
To assist management in evaluating and recommending appropriate policies and procedures to ensure the safeguard of assets, the reliability of the financial system, the adequacy of the internal controls and the performance of the operating units in accordance with management's overall profit objectives.

Cash and asset management
To control and optimize the utilization of corporate assets through effective cash, working capital and fixed capital control mechanisms.

EDP
To design, produce, implement, maintain and operate EDP systems for all corporate office functional areas; to consult and coordinate with division on large, companywide systems.

Alternatives

Once a decision unit's objective has been determined, analysis begins. The first step is to consider various ways of meeting the objective and to weigh the effect of these alternatives on the organization. Within an Accounting Department various alternatives should be proposed to carry out a specific decision unit's objective. Some examples of alternatives that have arisen during the authors' experiences follow:

Insurance
Proposal
Use an outside agency rather than internal staff.
Comment
Would be more expensive; slower follow-up on claims would result.

Treasury
Proposal
Combine treasury function with controller function.
Comment
The two functions have grown too large and complex to be managed well by one person.

Accounts receivable
Proposal
Acquire additional EDP facilities to improve speed of follow-up, handle increased work load, and to avoid hiring additional staff.
Comment
Would be expensive for present work load.

Decision unit managers within an Accounting Department should be encouraged to list many alternatives even if some seem inappropriate at the time. As the business volume of a company fluctuates, many of these alternatives may become feasible. For example, if a company's credit sales expand rapidly, the possibility of acquiring additional EDP facilities to improve collection speed would take on new significance.

Work load and performance measurements

Once the method of operation for a decision unit is selected, the incremental analysis begins. To evaluate the increments fairly, both the decision unit manager and his superiors need standards against which they can measure performance. Work load and performance measurements are generally easier to develop in accounting than in other departments because of accounting's need for record-keeping and its overall numbers orientation. Examples of work load and performance measurements are given:

Internal audit
Work load measurement: Cycle for audit coverage of reporting units.
Performance measurement: Frequency of monitoring recommended changes.

Accounts payable
Work load measurement: Delays in processing invoices.
Performance measurement: Value of accounts due in 60 days or less.

Accounts receivable
Work load measurement: Delays in follow-up of past due accounts.
Performance measurement: Value of accounts 60 days or more past due.

Costs and budgets

Work load measurement: Deadlines missed.

Performance measurement: Variance from forecast.

Increment determination

After appropriate work load and performance measurements are identified within a decision unit, the next step is to determine the various increments. This is the most critical analysis step. The manager must determine how he would operate at various budget levels. At a reduced budget level, should he reduce the work output of his decision unit, thus causing delays? Or should his decision unit perform the same work load at the expense of work quality? Or is there a suitable compromise of work load and quality?

Conversely, the decision unit manager must determine his priorities should his budget be increased. Since an Accounting Department is service oriented, the decision unit manager must be aware of his users' wants. Do they want faster service, better quality or something new?

Sample incremental analysis for insurance decision unit

1 of 4   Employ insurance manager and one clerk to provide survival level of insurance administration.

2 of 4   Add one claims administrator.

3 of 4   Add one workmen's compensation administrator.

4 of 4   Add one insurance analyst.

Sample incremental analysis for an EDP decision unit

1 of 4   Employ four people to maintain existing EDP systems.

2 of 4   Add one systems analyst programmer.

3 of 4   Add one Cobol programmer/analyst.

4 of 4   Add one junior programmer/data clerk for support of on-line data base maintenance.

Ranking

When ranking the increments of an Accounting Department, the ranking manager must be aware of any assumed interrelationships between decision units. For example, if the Insurance decision unit expects to use the services of a programmer from the EDP decision unit, the ranking manager must be sure that there is no misunderstanding. This type of integration can be dealt with if the ranking manager holds a group meeting where all decision unit managers discuss their increment structure and how the increments interrelate.

Special problems

The successful implementation of Zero-Base Planning and Budgeting to an Accounting Department encounters three special problems. These are discussed in a general fashion in Chapter 5.

1. Zero-Base Planning and Budgeting is often perceived as an accounting system rather than a planning system.

    To combat this perception, emphasis must be placed on the planning aspects, which are always tied to the budgeting process. This system merely structures and formalizes the connection.

2. Work load measurements and performance measurements are often thought to be the same thing. Consequently, quantitative measurements of results refer more often to quantity of work performed rather than quality of work performed.

    The differences between the two measurements should be explained. Decision unit managers should be encouraged to identify performance measurements since the quality of their work (e.g., number of forecast errors) is often more important than the quantity of their work (e.g., number of invoices processed).

3. Relating business volume assumptions to the Accounting Department work load is often difficult.

    If sales volume is expected to grow at 20 percent next year, what does this mean in terms of work load for the Accounts Payable decision unit or for the Insurance decision unit? It should be understood that even relatively large changes in volume do not affect accounting work load. If growth or decreases in revenue are significant special effort must be made to develop the impact upon accounting and the service it performs.

Results and benefits

Because accounting decision unit managers can think in terms of budgeting, implementation of the Zero-Base process is easier in an Accounting Department than in many other areas. For the same reason, however, accounting decision unit managers often do not analyze thoroughly. They are often so concerned with completing a budget and balancing the numbers that they do not consider carefully the important planning aspects of the process.

Once decision unit managers in an Accounting Department overcome this flaw, Zero-Base Planning and Budgeting is an effective tool for reallocating and controlling the overhead budget.

MANUFACTURING

Manufacturing Department budgets are unique within a company's budget framework. One category of manufacturing costs is that which is considered fixed throughout the relevant range of production for the upcoming year. Those fixed costs that are within the manager's control and budgeted by him on at least an annual basis (often referred to as managed costs) are appropriately analyzed by the Zero-Base approach.

However, many of the expenses incurred in a Manufacturing Department are variable or product costs which fluctuate directly with volume. These costs are budgeted through the standard cost process and are not appropriately evaluated by the Zero-Base Planning and Budgeting process.

Although not an all-inclusive list, the following categories of manufacturing overhead costs are usually classified as managed (and can be evaluated by the Zero-Base process):

Sample categories of manufacturing overhead costs

Supervision—Managers	Tool designers
Supervision—Foremen	Tool crib attendants
Industrial engineers	Crane operators
and mechanical engineers	Material handlers
Technical, secretarial,	Supplemental employee costs
clerical	Office supplies

Decision units

The above categories of cost will be found in a number of various types of Manufacturing departments. Generally, each currently existing department that prepares its own budget is a logical decision unit. Exceptions to this rule may very well develop, but use of the rule represents a good starting point. For a small Manufacturing Department, four or five decision units such as those shown below may suffice:

Administration
Product Planning
Quality Control
Shop Operations
Technical Services

For a larger Manufacturing Department (such as a plant site), a greater number of decision units encompassing more functions may be necessary. Such a list is provided in Table 3-4 at the end of the chapter.

Statements of objectives

The step following the identification of decision units is preparation of an objective statement for each of the decision units. In the manufacturing area the primary relationship to be established is the role of the decision unit in the product manufacturing process. Since each decision unit has a different supporting role, the nature of that support to other related departments needs to be specified.

In the manufacturing area, this interrelationship is extremely important. Changes in service levels in one department will often affect another plant area. Thus, the relationship established between the decision unit being analyzed and other departments or functions in the organization is of paramount importance.

Three examples of objectives statements follow:

Plant manager

To support the division through the plant management activity in accomplishing the manufacturing task for the Products and Components Plan.

Production control

To schedule and coordinate the activities of plant resources on a short term (four-month) basis in order to ship products when required by a customer and to enable efficient operation of the manufacturing organization.

Industrial engineering

To control manpower, equipment utilization, methods and costs; establish performance goals; provide timely manufacturing information and improve the effectiveness of manufacturing and support operations through sound industrial engineering practices.

Alternatives

During the next step in the process, that of developing alternatives to the current method of carrying out the decision unit's objective, a number of organizational issues and make-or-buy questions are raised. While a new operational method may not be adopted for the next year, other approaches are brought forth that are worth further study from a long-range planning standpoint. A separate program to integrate the study of these alternatives into a master review plan is often worthwhile.

Following is a list of alternatives developed for a forge shop and for a Technical Service group.

Forge shop

Proposals

a. Purchase forgings from outside source.
b. Manufacture dies on the outside.
c. Machine finished parts from bar stock forgings.
d. Subcontract all forging and finished parts machining.

Technical service

Proposals

a. Consolidate plant layout and electrical engineering groups.
b. Borrow plant layout and electrical engineering staff as needed from Division A.
c. Use outside service to meet tooling, equipment maintenance, and janitorial requirements.

Work load and performance measurements

After alternative operating methods have been developed and a method selected for the coming year (even if it is the current operating method), an evaluation of the standards by which to judge the effectiveness of each decision unit needs to be made. The Zero-Base Planning and Budgeting approach uses both work load and performance measurements to evaluate effectiveness.

Within a manufacturing organization, confusion sometimes arises between work load (as used in the Zero-Base Planning and Budgeting analysis) and production levels (which refer to the quantity of product output by the Production Department). For the analysis, the production level for each product or product line needs to be specified as part of the company plan for the forthcoming year. All decision unit managers then will base their department's service levels and capabilities on the desired productive output plan. The work load for a department may be specified either in terms of the plant's production goals or in terms of some other more satisfactory measure of demand upon the department.

Performance measurements are easiest to arrive at for those departments closest to the plant production departments since they can be related to output quality in terms of cost of rework or scrap, or efficiency.

Some typical work load and performance measurements for a Production Control Department, and Quality Control Department are given:

Production control

Work load measurement
a. Number of noncritical schedules.
b. Number of daily contacts with other service functions.
c. Number of new product prototypes introduced.

Performance measurement
a. Percent of schedule requirements met.

Quality control

Work load measurement
a. Net production direct labor hours.
b. Number of radiographic exposures.

Performance measurement
a. Code 613 items waiting for inspection (hours).
b. Number of postshipment deficiencies.
c. Dollar cost for correction of postshipment deficiencies.

The nature of the performance measurements will act as a guide for the development of service levels through preparation of the increment structure. Since any one department may have multiple responsibilities, the corporate plan and management emphasis for the forthcoming year dictate which activity within a department is of highest priority. Development of service levels within the manufacturing functional area can also involve a balancing act between the desired management depth, the level of technical service to be provided, the degree of process control sought, and the ability to expedite product on demand.

Increment determination

The increment structures developed for shop operations and technical services decision units are given below as examples.

Shop operations decision unit

1 of 6   Provide unevenly manned three-shift operation.
2 of 6   Add two section managers to allow for better supervision.

Shop operations decision unit (continued)

3 of 6   Add one crane crew.

4 of 6   Add material handlers.

5 of 6   Add material movement supervisor.

6 of 6   Add janitorial staff.

Technical services decision unit

1 of 5   Provide basic technical services.

2 of 5   Add mechanical engineer to second and third shifts.

3 of 5   Add welding engineer for tube welding.

4 of 5   Add stage two of preventive maintenance program.

5 of 5   Add shipping coordinator.

Ranking

The interrelationship between decision units is critical within the manufacturing organization. As is true for certain other functional areas, the ranking of decision unit increments is best carried out jointly by the decision unit managers and their superior, the ranking manager. Should conditions within the organization prevent or caution against a participative ranking, the ranking manager should, at the very least, consult with his decision unit managers in a group meeting to understand the interrelationships prior to ranking the increments himself. A ranking of the increments shown in the table below shows how one organization valued the relative importance of various managed cost activities within the manufacturing area.

While the above discussion has focused on the application of Zero Base to managed costs, it can also be applied to certain product costs—namely, those that are indirect product costs with funding flexibility at any given production level, at least in the short run. The funding flexibility generally arises through increased efficiency,

TABLE 3-1
Ranking table for Manufacturing

Rank and department		Services
1. Shop Operations	1 of 6	Provide unevenly manned three-shift operation.
2. Production Planning	1 of 5	Provide minimal production services.
3. Technical Service	1 of 5	Provide basic technical service.
4. Administration	1 of 1	Supervision and administration.
5. Production Planning	2 of 5	Add staff for additional work-in-process expediting.
6. Production Planning	3 of 5	Add staff for additional long range of learning.
7. Production Planning	4 of 5	Add scheduling clerk.
8. Shop Operations	2 of 6	Add two section managers.
9. Shop Operations	3 of 6	Add one crane crew.
10. Shop Operations	4 of 6	Add material handlers.
11. Technical Service	2 of 5	Add mechanical engineer to second and third shifts.
12. Shop Operations	5 of 6	Add material movement supervisor.
13. Technical Service	3 of 5	Add welding engineer for tube welding.
14. Technical Service	4 of 5	Add stage two of preventive maintenance program.
15. Technical Service	5 of 5	Add shipping coordinator.
16. Shop Operations	6 of 6	Add janitorial staff.
17. Production Planning	5 of 5	Add additional expediter.

reduced waste, or modified performance. Cost categories such as maintenance, shop supplies, rework and scrap, testing, hand tools, and utilities are frequently subjected to a Zero-Base Planning and Budgeting analysis, although not classified as managed costs.

Results and benefits

The use of Zero-Base Planning and Budgeting for managed costs and for indirect product costs should result in a number of organizational benefits, including:

1. Improved effectiveness for the manufacturing overhead dollars expended.
2. Greater awareness of any short-term volume relationships that may be present for the overhead costs.
3. Improved understanding of the relationship of spending levels of support departments to those of manufacturing departments.
4. Evaluation of alternative methods of operations and the implementation of further study of those deemed worthwhile.
5. A greater involvement of line management in the planning and decision-making process.
6. Stabilization or reduction in the applied overhead charge rate.
7. Improved communications between top plant management and department managers at all levels.

ENGINEERING

The application of the Zero-Base process to an Engineering Department requires added preparation during the initial stages of the process. The benefits, however, have proven to be substantial, especially in regard to manager training and cost reallocation.

Decision units

Engineering Department decision units may be identified as either specific projects or programs; or functional organizational units. Identification of decision units as projects may be the best choice where project management responsibility, as well as technological responsibility and understanding, is centralized. This approach may be used, for example, where control over budget, project workflow and technological performance variables are under the responsibility of one person. However, technological responsibility is usually distributed widely throughout the organization. In such cases, a better planning and budgeting result may be achieved if decision units are defined on a functional basis.

The following is typical of functionally oriented decision units. In each case, they correspond to an already existing organizational unit.

Field evaluation   Service project engineering
Application engineering   Technology development

Statements of objectives

The complexity of engineering related tasks, especially in a large multifunctional Engineering Department, requires an accurate statement of decision unit objective or purpose.

Clarity and mission orientation is necessary for the thorough analysis of decision unit activities and the development of meaningful performance measures. Sample statements of objective follow:

Field evaluation
> To provide engineering information and data on the thermodynamic performance of turbines once they are installed and operating.

Service project engineering
> To provide and/or coordinate all engineering services subsequent to the delivery and acceptance of the equipment by the customer.

Application engineering
> To provide marketing and technical information for sales proposals, on competitive position and product line, and to provide expected performance data to customers.

Technology development
> To develop and update the technology base required to support the design of efficient and reliable turbines.

Regardless of how decision units are chosen, the precise and accurate determination of the business volume assumption or work load determinants is a prerequisite for the ultimate success of the analysis. Decision unit managers must know in fairly specific terms what is expected of them in order to establish the cost/benefit relationship at the various levels of service. They can then begin to adopt the perspective of a businessman who must allocate scarce resources to activities of varying priority instead of that of a technician primarily concerned with the optimal performance of certain tasks. Once decision unit managers begin to focus on results rather than activities, they frequently develop more creative approaches toward meeting their objectives and discover ways to improve overall efficiency.

When the objective of the decision unit is established and the work load determinant established for each decision unit, the decision unit manager should develop and explore alternative ways of achieving the decision unit's objective.

Alternatives

In a capital, technology-intensive industry or company, the ability of decision unit managers to develop realistic alternatives is limited—especially alternatives that are within their authority to implement.

The historical commitment to a particular manufacturing process or technology limits the range of alternatives open to decision unit managers. Nevertheless, managers should be encouraged to make an effort to develop new ways of achieving their objectives which could then be studied for possible implementation. Especially fruitful are ideas which involve organizational change or realignment. Frequently, the lower-middle level of managers is aware of organizational realignment which can promote improved workflow and efficiency.

Work load and performance measurements

Before performing the incremental analysis, the decision unit manager must develop performance and work load measurements which can be used at each level of service to measure progress toward meeting the unit's objective. The manager should be able to choose measurements which reflect both quality and quantity improvements at each level of service.

A sample work load and performance measurements in Engineering decision units is given:

Field evaluations
Work load measurement
a.   Projects oriented toward verifying design configurations.

Performance measurement
a.   Number of ASME tests conducted.
b.   Number of customer-conducted tests witnessed.

Service project engineering
Work load measurement
a.   Service order projections from marketing department.
b.   Historically based projection of the number and magnitude of major breakdowns.
c.   Actual number of service orders currently being processed.

Performance measurement
a.   Number of service orders supported.
b.   Number of customer service requests answered.
c.   Backlog of service requests.

Application engineering
Work load measurement
a.   Marketing plans from the marketing department.
b.   Actual orders on the books.

Performance measurement
a.   Number of negotiations supported.
b.   Number and depth of competitive position reviews.
c.   Turnaround time of customer requests.

Technology development
Work load measurement
a.   Output called for from outgoing strategic projects.
b.   Estimated number of major design failures.

Performance measurement

a. Time variance from strategic work plan.

b. Number and type of active projects handled.

Most of the performance measurements chosen reflect performance against quantity measurements. This is due to the task-oriented nature of the engineering function and, in part, to the feeling among engineers that quality is not a variable to be managed like cost or time. Engineers feel that the marginal cost of lower quality is far greater than any potential savings. It is difficult to test that assumption because of the lag between the time when the engineering work is done and the time when the consequences of less complete engineering become evident. However, if the firm's internal project management system calls for good documentation of time and technical performance variables, the decision unit manager will be able to develop performance measurements which satisfactorily address quality.

The balance between quality and quantity must be continually managed during the incremental analysis. The lack of a good internal project management system becomes evident when decision unit managers are unable to confront the question: "With additional resources should I perform additional tasks, do the ones I'm currently doing better, or a little of both?"—because good planning information is not available. The decision unit manager should have a portfolio of "investment" options available to him at each level of service to compare through cost/benefit analysis.

Increment determinations

Much of the training benefit of Zero-Base Planning and Budgeting occurs during the incremental analysis. During this phase, the manager is required to assign relative values and priorities to activities which he previously felt were indispensable. The manager frequently feels that he still must do everything—that even at a first increment level of activity, management would still hold him accountable for doing all that he is currently doing. This problem can be minimized in two ways: (1) the manager reorients management's expectation through a good analysis tied together by sound performance measures; and (2) management supports the process by demanding precise analysis and adjusting expectations of what can realistically be accomplished at each level of service.

A summarization of the increment structure for two decision units follows. It provides good examples of what may realistically be expected at various levels of service as well as examples of the need to consider both quality and quantity.

Incremental analysis of an Engineering Department

Field evaluation

1 of 4   Perform tests already scheduled for 1976 in order to support planned service engineering program.

2 of 4   Plan 1977 test schedule and respond to unscheduled breakdowns to develop data for improving design.

3 of 4   More extensive analysis of test results and new testing methods development to allow service engineering to schedule planned shutdowns for improved customer service level.

4 of 4   Systematic planning and analysis of field testing to add data to technology reservoir in support of development engineering's long range design improvement programs.

Service project engineering

1 of 4   Prepare service orders for major breakdowns. Answer customer requests on large equipment in use ten years or more to maintain a good corporate image with 80 percent of customer base.

2 of 4   Support litigation activities and customer requests on medium-sized equipment; schedule planned equipment shutdown for maintenance.

3 of 4   Expand preventative maintenance service program to enhance image and avoid costly repairs of breakdowns.

4 of 4   Support manufacturing on service order related production problems to eliminate delays in production process and improve customer service level.

Ranking

Once the incremental analyses have been fully developed, departmental management is responsible for ranking the increments. There are two important elements to consider when ranking the increments of an Engineering Department: (1) the functional interrelationships which are usual in most engineering organizations must be formally considered so that departmental "balance" is maintained at each level of service; (2) changes in the firm's business and product mix or marketing emphasis must be recognized in order to assure that the proper product lines or markets are receiving engineering support.

The first element is dealt with by appropriate structuring of the ranking meeting and management of the ranking process. At the ranking each manager should make a brief presentation to explain his rationale for his incremental analysis. He should also present an analysis of any interdepartmental relationships. He should describe at each level of service the inputs which are necessary for the functioning of his decision unit as well as the outputs which are critical to the operation of the other functional units. This round table analysis can be more or less formal, depending on the complexity of the organization.

Once the ranking manager understands the nature of the interrelationships he may proceed to rank the department guided by continuing input from the decision unit managers or lower level ranking managers.

There is a natural check and balance built into this ranking process which provides two benefits: an accurate analysis of each functional unit's dependence on and contribution to other functional units is provided, thereby minimizing the possibility that a decision unit will get funding without justifying the statement that "other departments depend on me"; and sensitive or critical areas where it would be destructive to reduce costs are readily identified.

The second factor to consider—recognition of changing product line or market emphasis—is addressed by assuring that engineering management has received clear, long-term planning guidelines from top management. Because short-term budgeting decisions may have longer term impact, engineering management must be able to integrate longer term operational requirements into its short-term planning strategy.

The ranking example in Table 3-2 shows how one engineering manager reflected his company's adjustment to changing market conditions through the ranking process. In this case the market for new equipment was maturing and stagnating while the demand for service and modernization of existing equipment was increasing.

An analysis of this ranking shows that management emphasized the improvement of service capabilities at the expense of application engineering and the development of new technology.

TABLE 3-2
Ranking table for Engineering Department

Rank and decision unit	Increment
1. Service project engineering	1 of 4
2. Field evaluation	1 of 4
3. Application engineering	1 of 4
4. Technology development	1 of 4
5. Field evaluation	2 of 4
6. Application engineering	2 of 4
7. Service project engineering	2 of 4
8. Service project engineering	3 of 4
9. Field evaluation	3 of 4
10. Service project engineering	4 of 4
11. Application engineering	3 of 4
12. Field evaluation	4 of 4
13. Technology development	2 of 3
14. Application engineering	4 of 4
15. Technology development	3 of 3

Results and benefits

Although the implementation of Zero-Base Planning and Budgeting requires extra effort during the preparation stage, especially with respect to decision unit identification and the establishment of the business volume assumption or work load, general management as well as all levels of engineering management can expect significant benefits from the process.

Because the Zero-Base process enables general management to deal with units of reasonable size, management is able to gain better insight into the overall engineering activity. Improving the communication between general and engineering management is especially important in those cases where general management's background is nontechnical.

Through the ranking process engineering management may be assured not only of aligning the overall engineering efforts to mesh with the organization's business needs, but also of balancing the functional engineering activities within the overall engineering effort.

The analyses submitted by individual decision unit managers also allow upper level management to evaluate the decision unit manager's understanding of his objectives and their relationship to higher level organizational objectives. The result of this evaluation may be an ongoing dialogue among various levels of engineering management leading to improved management within the department.

Frequently the most important result is that the decision unit manager develops a more accurate understanding of and/or appreciation for his contribution to those engineering or business systems with which he works.

MARKETING

When Zero-Base Planning and Budgeting is applied effectively in a Marketing Department, the results are meaningful to all levels of management. A major reason is the type of performance measurement that is relevant for evaluating Marketing decision units.

Performance measurements for many nonmarketing decision units are not dollar oriented and, consequently, the impact of more (or less) engineering projects, more (or less) customer complaints, and longer (or shorter) delays in processing invoices must be interpolated to reflect dollar consequences. However, the most common performance measurements for Marketing decision units are dollar oriented, which greatly simplify cost/benefit comparisons.

The advantage that the Zero-Base process brings to a Marketing Department is that these performance measurements may be incorporated within a structured planning process. Traditionally, performance measurements such as "contribution margin" have been used in Marketing Departments only to evaluate potential increases or decreases from the current level of operations. The Zero-Base process provides for application of these measurements—not from the current level of operations—but from an unconstrained starting point. All Marketing Department operations, both existing and new, are evaluated before any funding decisions are made.

It should be noted, however, that although top management relates best to dollar-oriented performance measurements, these measurements pose certain problems for them. The most significant one centers on the generation of accurate numbers. For example, the decision to hire an additional salesman within a Marketing Department may very well depend on the incremental revenues and profits that he would achieve. The generation of accurate revenue and profit figures can only be close approximations at best. Top management therefore needs to scrutinize these figures carefully before making a funding decision.

Another point to consider is that an enterprising sales manager may exaggerate the expected benefits associated with an additional salesman in an effort to win top management approval. Also, the impact of an additional salesman will be felt not only in the upcoming year, but in future years as well. Top management needs to consider the long-term impact, realizing that the accuracy of revenue and profit estimates becomes increasingly dubious the longer the projections.

Decision unit identification

Identifying appropriate decision units in a Marketing Department is crucial. Should there be one corporate sales decision unit or several regional sales decision units? Should Advertising and Publicity be considered as one decision unit or should they be analyzed separately? The size of the Marketing Department will oftentimes be the main determinant for answering these questions. Other times, the particular characteristics of an organization must be considered before determining the appropriate decision units.

Some typical decision units in a Marketing Department are listed below:

Sales   Marketing Services
Advertising   Publicity
Distribution   Order Entry

Statements of objectives

Since a Marketing decision unit may be broad or narrow, determined by the organization's size and characteristics, a clear statement of objective takes on great importance. It is with this statement that higher levels of management will gear their analytical thought process and eventual funding decisions. Poorly written statements of objectives will result in long delays in completing analyses as well as the greater risk of making inappropriate funding decisions.

Some statements of objectives for Marketing decision units are shown below:

Corporate sales
To achieve domestic sales performance such that present customers receive satisfactory service, gross revenues increase by 12 percent, new customer sales increase by 20 percent, and contribution margin of salesmen be at least double the cost of salesmen.

Advertising and promotion
To promote sales of company products via literature, direct customer mail, trade publicity, trade literature, and trade shows.

Marketing services
To provide management with market research, planning, development, and control data relating to product sales.

Alternatives

The Marketing Department intertwines the planning and budgeting process more than most other departments. There are various modes of running a Marketing Department and these modes should be reviewed periodically for their appropriateness.

Alternatives within Marketing decision units often have more impact on an organization's operations than alternatives within most other areas. A few alternatives that might be considered when analyzing a Marketing decision unit follow.

Corporate sales
Organize by market segment instead of by geography.

Advertising
Instead of an in-house staff, use the services of an outside advertising agency for all space advertising, promotion, and publicity.

Order entry
Greater computer application to the existing manual order entry system.

Marketing decision unit managers need to review their alternatives periodically, since previously discarded choices may suddenly become appropriate as an organization's environment and/or fortunes change.

For example, advertising strategy for a particular product line will likely change as the product line moves from a stage of growth to a stage of maturity.

Work load and performance measurements

After alternative operating modes are compared with current operations, the desired mode for next year's operations is chosen and the incremental analysis begins. The increment structure within a Marketing Department is based largely on top management guidelines.

A policy emphasizing short-term profitability will lead to a different increment structure from one emphasizing long-term growth. To evaluate the importance of funding specific increments, identification of appropriate work load and performance measurements is essential. Some common measurements for Marketing decision units follow:

Sales
Work load measurement
a. Number of customer contracts per month.

Performance measurement
a. Contribution margin.
b. Sales volume.

Order entry
Work load measurement
a. Backlog in processing.

Performance measurement
a. Number of entry errors per month.

Distribution
Work load measurement
a. Delivery delays.

Performance measurement
a. Lost customers due to slow deliveries.

Promotion

Work load measurement
a.   Number of trade shows.

Performance measurement
a.   New customers generated by trade shows.

Increment determination

After identifying the key measurement for his decision unit, the manager must then construct increments that maximize the derived benefits of his budget while adhering to the policy guidelines issued by top management. Sample increment structures for a Sales decision unit and an Advertising and Promotion decision unit are presented below:

Regional Sales

1 of 4   Employ a regional sales manager, three salesmen to cover the eight state Midwest region, one service technician, and one secretary.

2 of 4   Add one salesman, realigning territories.

3 of 4   Add one service technician, providing quicker and more effective customer service.

4 of 4   Add one salesman, allowing for better territory coverage and a stronger base to achieve long-term growth.

Advertising and Promotion

1 of 4   Employ one advertising manager to coordinate all planning, creation and execution of company advertising and promotion. Funds should be budgeted for brochures, price lists, and promotional materials.

2 of 4   Fund $25,000 to provide for space advertising in major trade journals.

3 of 4   Hire a knowledgeable inside publicist to design and implement ongoing publicity programs.

4 of 4   Fund $12,000 to allow for exhibiting at six trade shows annually.

Ranking

Ranking Marketing decision units requires a thorough understanding of the interrelationships between decision units, as well as a keen awareness by the ranking manager to ensure that all increment structures were designed in accordance with top management's guidelines.

The Marketing ranking manager must review each set of increments carefully to ensure that the dollar-oriented performance measurements are credible. Sales managers, as we have shown previously, may wittingly or unwittingly overstate the benefits to be derived from additional salesmen. The ranking manager must be watchful of any such "optimism" if he is to put together a logical priority-ordered ranking.

Table 3-3 shows a sample ranking table for a Marketing Department.

Conclusions

The effective application of the process to a Marketing Department requires the following:

1. Dollar-oriented performance measurements must be scrutinized carefully. Sales managers may overstate the impact of reducing or adding salesmen for reasons of defensiveness and/or optimism.

2. Zero-Base Planning and Budgeting concentrates on the upcoming year's operations. However, the impact of funding certain increments may be felt more in later years; hence, long-term effects of budget reductions or expansions must be considered.

3. The interrelationship between decision units must be understood. For example, an expected sales growth of 15 percent may be based on an assumed level of advertising and promotion. To give a high rank to a sales increment that promises greater sales growth while giving a low rank to the associated advertising and promotion increment would lead to an ineffective operating plan.

Zero-Base Planning and Budgeting provides Marketing decision unit managers with a meaningful approach for planning next year's operations. It has proven itself to be effective at all management levels in a Marketing Department.

TABLE 3-3
Ranking table for a Marketing Department

Rank	Decision unit increments	Increment number	1977 Proposed (a) Expense ($000)	(b) Em-ployees	1977 Cumulative (a) Expense ($000)	(b) Em-ployees	1976 Forecast (a) Expense ($000)	(b) Em-ployees	Percent change (1977 − 1976 × 100) (a) Expense ($000)	(b) Em-ployees	Notes
1	Eastern Region Sales	1 of 4	140	7	140	7	168	9	35	35	1 manager; 4 sales-men; 2 clerks
2	Western Region Sales	1 of 4	118	6	258	13	135	8	64	65	1 manager; 3 sales-men; 2 clerks
3	Advertising and Promotion	1 of 3	35	—	273	13	47	—	73	65	Brochures and basic promotion
4	Marketing Administration	1 of 2	44	2	337	15	51	3	84	75	Director; secretary
5	Eastern Region Sales	2 of 4	23	1	360	16			90	80	1 salesman
6	Advertising and Promotion	2 of 3	15	—	375	16			94	80	4 trade journal ads per year
7	Eastern Region Sales	3 of 4	13	1	388	17			97	85	1 clerk
8	Western Region Sales	2 of 4	13	1	401	18			100	90	1 clerk
9	Marketing Administration	2 of 2	11	1	412	19			103	95	1 clerk
10	Advertising and Promotion	3 of 3	15	—	427	19			106	95	4 more trade journal ads per year
11	Eastern Region Sales	4 of 4	23	1	450	20			112	100	1 salesman
12	Western Region Sales	3 of 4	21	1	471	21			117	105	1 salesman
13	Western Region Sales	4 of 4	21	1	492	22			123	110	1 salesman
	Total				492	22	401	20			

TABLE 3-4
Examples of objectives, performance categories, and measurements

Category	Area	Objective	Performance category	Measurement
I	Accounts receivable	To process data in such a manner that we collect our receivables as quickly as possible without undue customer irritation.	Number of customer accounts requiring monthly adjustments. Average number of days to collect.	350 65
I	Corporate payroll	To pay employees accurately and on time, record expenses and taxes and control the cost of these operations in the most efficient manner possible.	Accuracy of reporting. Unfavorable feedback from other departments. Payroll dates missed. Report deadlines missed.	100% None 100% None
I	Accounts payable	Prompt processing of Corporate Head Office and mill vendor invoices for timely payment and accurate capture of financial information.	More variety in functions (percent of time spent on primary function). More accurate input. Chargeback for unearned discount. Overtime expense and temporary help. Invoice volume.	53% 99% $200 $3,400 $72,000
I	Capital expenditure accounting	Ensure proper accounting controls and reports for the administration of the Capital Request and Expenditure program. Provide centralized computer accounting and necessary guidance to operating units related to reporting of all Corporate property.	Quick response to policy inquiries avoiding costly wrong action by units. Timeliness of Property Ledger distribution.	50% 60%
I	General ledger	Timely and accurate preparation of the Head Office General Ledger for input to Corporate financial statements. Provide accounting services to Corporate Staff Departments.	Type of analysis. Loss—no audit of employee expense reports. Expense reports audited. Outside audit expense.	None $2,000 0 $3,000
I	Financial statements and analysis	Prepare and provide top management, directors, shareowners, governmental agencies, and the financial community accurate (and on a timely basis) consolidated financial statements of the corporation, in conjunction therewith, perform and provide detailed analyses and reports (routinely, and at special request) to management external auditors applicable to those statements.	Consolidation and analyses (days delay). Accuracy of statements and analytical work. Dependence on outside auditors for analyses now "in-house." Special project work and analyses requested. Required assistance to newly acquired units.	3 85% $2,000 75% 20%

Function	Description	Measure
Corporate accounting	To provide management and coordinate work efforts for the Corporate Accounting Department and to develop accounting procedures and accounting treatment (for special situations) in conjunction with the four working supervisors. (Financial Accounting, Financial Statements, and Analyses, Capital Expenditures and Property, and Salary Payroll sections.)	Errorless statements and reports. 90% Develop accounting treatment for special situations. 75% Errorless accounting period closings. 12
Accounting	To handle all accounting for the International Department, including payment of invoices, billing, corrections, financial statements, analysis and consulting.	Invoice payments. 1,500 per week Late payments of invoices. 25% Incorrect amounts paid. 30%
Accounts receivable, national accounts and U.S. government	To collect accounts receivable due from National Accounts and U.S. Government.	Collection letters on unpaid invoices sent when invoices are 20 and 40 days old. 30% Reminders sent on past due service charge invoices. 80%
General accounting	To record, process and analyze data affecting accounts of departments and report results to management, government agencies, and stockholders on a timely basis.	Financial statement preparation in work days. 16 Variance from profit plan of over $1,000 per month—number of accounts. 45 Account analysis per month. 50
Adjustments	To handle agent request for adjustments relative to bill of lading charges in an accurate, efficient and expeditious manner.	Annual number of adjustments handled. 152,000 Average number of days to handle adjustment request. 30 Average monthly backlog of adjustments to be handled. 8,000
Rates and tariffs	To provide a complete tariff service at highest possible level and to eliminate costly and time consuming correspondence and phone calls from shippers with respect to improper tariff charges and handle time-consuming tariff matters for other departments to eliminate distractions for them and assure that quality tariff work is accomplished.	Tariff notification publications. 130 Correspondence. 300 Phone calls. 150 Tariff publications. 2
Quality assurance	To assist customers, outside government agencies, and company agents in resolving problems that cannot be serviced by agents on local level; this includes refunding of charges when necessary and covers all types of complaints on all services with the exception of loading delays, claims for loss, damage and delay related expenses.	Number of complaints serviced, per month. 8 Percent of telephone complaints serviced the same day. 96 Percent of error in judgments. 80 Follow-up time on active files. 2 weeks Written communication response time. 2 days

TABLE 3-4 (continued)

Category	Area	Objective	Performance category	Measurement
II	Regional service	To provide expert servicing of equipment in a customer's plant. To provide services at a customer's plant that help our sales effort so that we can provide total capability.	Call back by customer per month. Billings. Days delay on emergency calls. Service credit.	2% 135,000 1/2 70,000
II	(Sales)	Sell and service customers and prospects. Build company image as a systems supplier, improve image as a preferred instrument supplier, get specified on projects.	Sales coverage. Ability to penetrate systems market—present and future. Sales revenues. Chance of customer retention. Percent of available business.	Fair Fair 475,000 Fair 60%
II	(Sales)	Sell to and service customers. Prime purpose is to be sure oil, gas and chemical companies come to think of us as a preferred supplier of instrumentation, systems and backup service. Secondary and concurrent objective is to work with, and obtain favorable and preferred consideration from Engineering Contractor/Consultants by combating competition well intrenched in region.	Sales coverage. Ability to penetrate systems market—present and future. Sales revenues. Chance of customer retention. Percent of available business obtained.	Fairly good Good 700,000 Good 75%
II	Service	To provide demand and contract and sales support service and training with a cost of sales of 75% or better, to obtain long term service on new projects and in existing plants.	Service coverage. Delay on emergencies. Service revenues. Customer retention. Opportunity for large projects (influence).	Good Small 55,000 90% 20%
II	Western region	To represent and sell products and expertise to existing customers and to build a base such that sales for and beyond 1977 will continue to expand.	Order entry delays (days). Territory coverage. Order entry ($000).	2 Good $1,040
II	Region sales	To sell product and services in area and to decision makers in area where product is for use in other areas. To enhance the reputation of the company by providing the right product, on time, in a competent manner, thus leading to future sales.	Complaints from production department per month. Complaints from customers per month. Orders. Average days delay for order entry. Customer coverage (percent).	4 6 3,303,000 3 76

	Function	Objective	Measures	Value
=	Sales	To market and sell products in industries such that our sales grow and our market share increases at the same time meeting company objectives, to establish us as a credible supplier for major expansions and grass roots projects.	Sales coverage. Self sufficiency. Sales revenues. Opportunity for large projects.	Very good Very good $2,500,000 30%
=	Technical sales department	Interpret customer requirements, make quotations, enter orders and log progress through department. Prepare Unit Order Budget and discounted-order analysis. Maintain and distribute catalog and price list material. Investigate credit requests and initiate credit advice where applicable.	Days delay in coding. Days delay in order entry.	1 3
=	Projects and proposals . . .	*Projects.* To complete both technically and commercially all aspects of a project to the satisfaction of company and our customer. *Proposals.* To provide high-quality technical and commercial proposals generally in the product lines which will generate further interest amongst our clients enabling more large contracts to be secured.	Projects. Proposals.	16 19
=	"A" unit production control	Plan, organize, direct, coordinate, and control the orderly flow of equipment components through the manufacturing processes of fabrication, machine, assembly, and shipment; the goal being delivery of a complete product, on time, in accordance with shop schedules, financial planning, and customer requirements.	On time delivery performance: (1) Service orders (2) Shop orders Service to shop as a function of net allowed hours. Productivity.	92% 91.8% 103% 76.5%
=	Expediting, factory loading and customer service . . .	To ensure that the manufacturing unit is supplied with the proper parts and in quantities to load the shop to its maximum utility. To keep track of all orders so as to be able to answer customer and staff enquiries and to devote the effort to reduce schedules when customer needs must be met or staff information must be provided.	Customer complaints. Staff complaints. Shipments on time. Improve cost of sales.	10 10 80% 1
=	Scheduling and write-up . .	To process the product order as received from Sales so that a delivery date satisfactory to the customer can be set for all product whether purchased or manufactured. To convert customer order into breakdown in line with manufacturing procedures to initiate provision or required parts to factory and list of parts for manufacturing the work-in-process orders.	Customer complaints. Backlog of work (days).	10 5

TABLE 3-4 (continued)

Cate-gory	Area	Objective	Performance category	Measurement
II	Purchasing	To place orders and monitor the receiving and invoicing of all material from all sources except affiliates.	Delivery falldowns. Delay in entering orders (days).	2% 1/2 to 2
II	Regional office	To perform demand and contract service for customers at their plant or repair their instruments in our shop, plus troubleshoot and correct faulty instruments, check out, calibrate, modify instruments from stock for emergency situations. Build a good rapport with customers and a good reputation of expertise and after sales service and pay for itself.	Ability to respond to customer service requirements. Percent of service business turned down. Service billings (income). Service credit. Days delay for emergency calls.	Fair 40 55,000 16,000 1-2 weeks
III	F.I.S.	To receive, store, update, prepare and issue manufacturing information to division manufacturing. This includes work documents, change notices, "G" sheets, EANs and the supply of all drawings. In addition the unit is to be organized to control the release of CPSL information, expedite the orders, report all known promise dates, material completion, and shipment information in an effort to provide better customer service and the input and control of Work-in-Process inventory records to develop and satisfy the operating strategic system concept.	Overdue (3% of 30 orders at 1,000) items per order. Manufacturing Information Processing.	900 24 hours
III	Manufacturing operations—management	Manage the manufacturing operations and the associated services which include the manufacturing engineering, production control, industrial engineering, tool planning, design and engineering and numerical control programming functions to meet financial objectives by shipping steam turbine components on time, highest quality and at least cost.	Unresolved union problems (increased number of work stoppages). Decline in work habits. Productivity. Net allowed hours. Possible delays in shipments including critical service work.	Some problems extend next day. Some loss. 73% 97% Slight delays into next month.

	Function	Objective	Measure	Value
III	Industrial engineering	To minimize and control manufacturing costs for plant manufacturing areas.	Upgrading of lineups—number of detailed lineups generated.	2,600
			Time standard verification effort—time studies conducted.	0
			Manpower effort expended on nonstandard control (percent).	Nil
			Productivity problem identification—surveys and studies.	4
			Cost improvement effort—dollars accepted for unit.	$1,577,000
III	Service products	Receive schedule, and prepare division commitment dates for service orders; then control, coordinate, and expedite them through the division to reduce forced and scheduled outage times. Report to Division Management, Division Service, and Customer representatives, the status of all service orders in support of the division's sales plan.	Repair orders—number of orders versus ontime performance.	485—79%
			Renewal Parts Orders. Ontime performance.	6,000—71%
			Order status reporting.	No
			Average customer outage time.	2 weeks
III	Inventory control	To monitor inventory levels for all parts and finished product and place orders for all material required for customers and factory orders.	Ordering backlog (days).	6-18
			Increase in stockouts due to ordering problems.	25%
			Reverse in number of major product codes reviewed.	2-3
III	Stockroom	To maintain the physical stock for all customer orders and to fill parts to customer orders or to factory orders. To maintain the stock of factory supply expensed items and requisition same as required. Minimize customer forced and/or scheduled outage times through the management service orders through the scheduling and preparation of commitment dates and expedition of the service orders through division manufacturing.	Turnaround time (days).	4-8
			Increase in filling errors.	3-4 times
IV	Administration	a. To perform all phases of personnel so as to create the best possible working relationship between employee and management. b. To supervise seven employees of the Central Service function to service all other decision units of the company.	Telexing delays.	1/2 hour
			Cafeteria delays.	3 min.
			Internal mail pickup and delivery.	100%
			Typing, filing, copying, billing.	100%
			Telex backup.	100%
			Switchboard backup.	75%
			Personnel duties.	100%
			Group insurance and workmen's compensation.	100%
IV	EDP	To provide management with a fast and reliable M.I.S. To transform management and user's needs and requirements into workable and manageable systems.	Massive improvement.	100%
			Professional competence.	150%
			Programs implemented.	80
			Projects done.	13

TABLE 3-4 (concluded)

Category	Area	Objective	Performance category	Measurement
IV	Systems	a. Provide data control and data entry services to interface between information from functional areas and the computer. b. Analyze the present system with the objective of resolving problems to provide the best and most economical results. c. To plan future systems.	Accuracy of reports. Turnaround time.	95 .6 weeks (3 days)
IV	Administration	To produce a manufactured product economically, to the level of quality and service required by our customers and within agreed delivery schedules. To investigate all capital expenditures and supervise those approved by management to create and maintain a system and atmosphere as required to achieve this object.	Customer complaints. Personnel relations. Amount of nonproductive labor and overtime due to problems. Weeks for shipments.	10 1 3 8
V	Numerical control department	To accurately develop numerical control programs to produce control tapes, plots, and numerical computer manuscripts for the operation of all numerical control machine tools.	Number of N/C tape programs produced per requirement. N/C tapes checked for quality and correctness. Family type N/C program development. Programs for other departments.	100% 100% 80% 80%
V	Manufacturing engineering	Support production in the unit by outlining manufacturing methods for high-pressure boiler feed pump and low-pressure steam turbines. Also supply technical advice that encompasses two-way information flow between operations and engineering on current product. Also to define with other manufacturing engineering personnel design objectives on future products or redesign.	Shop problems solved by Manufacturing, Engineering. Development projects completed/expenditure. Cost improvement assignments. Operator qualification. Manufacturing instructions—Lester (MIL).	70% 30 projects, $138,000 $1,103,900 50% 80
V	Tool planning and design	To add to the profitability of the division through the planning, design, and development of the tooling needs of the division as well as provide technical support for the cost improvement, quality assurance, and safety programs.	Tool planning and design coverage (rated 0 to 100) 1,500 drawings per year. Q.A. coverage (rated 0 to 100). Cost improvement effort (rated 0 to 100) $250,000 Bogie. Shop problems (number per week)—delay. Coverage-lineups, tickets, P.O., tool cards, filing (number per week).	70 20 30 20 250

∨	No. 1 and No. 3 Shop manufacturing	Layout machine and fit Inner Cylinders and Inlet Exhaust Cylinders on Turbines.	Management ratio/Elap./NAH (K). 76/184.5/140.2 Lost time due to crane delays, hours per dollar (K). 0.7/5.0 Overtime to cover low productivity (K). 2.2/8.1 PLV due to low productivity. 16.1 Total of these measures this increment. 26.2
∨	No. 2 Shop and S-Building manufacturing	Layout machine fit and blade all rotors in No. 2 shop. Also weld and hydrotest cylinders.	Management ratio/Elap./NAH (K). 75.5./380.1/28 Losttime due to crane delay, hours per dollar (K). 2.5/18.3 Overtime to cover low-productivity elapse per $. 2.3/8.4 PLV due to above. 16.8

			Expense	Employees
∨	Product engineering	To monitor and inspect goods that are shipped to all customers. To analyze problems and to suggest ways and means of solving these problems. To maintain and upgrade if necessary own Q/A, Q/C program so that our product will enhance our position in the marketplace.	One inspector and 1 senior product engineer. 30,529	2
			Add 1 product engineer. 46,248	3
			Add 1 product engineer. This is current level. 61,747	4
∨	Control panel design	Translate customer supplied information into working drawings of customer control panels, and purchase material for same to forward to our Panel Shop for assembly. Provide backup services for our Sales and Engineering Department.	Amount of panel support. $530,000	
∨	Systems engineering	To provide technical expertise to customers (especially sales department). To upgrade and administer training courses for personnel and customers. To provide an on-going technical liaison with regional office.	Quality would improve because all staff would have more time for each operation. There could be a reduction in delays due to adding this unit but no way to measure. 85%	

Note: Categories: I. Finance/Legal Accounting; II. Sales/Marketing/Distribution; III. Production/Operations; IV. Administration/EDP; V. Engineering.

4

Case illustrations
of Zero-Base
Planning and Budgeting

Bridging the span between the theoretical and the real is the goal in this presentation of several cases selected from the authors' experiences. Detailed descriptions of six Zero-Base Planning and Budgeting implementations in case format appear in the Appendix at the end of the book. Five cases were chosen from the authors' work with Zero Base; a sixth has been selected from Harvard Business School teaching cases.

A brief summary of each of the first five cases, along with a perspective of their similar and disparate characteristics, will be presented in an indexlike approach to the complete case descriptions. This chapter may be used as a guide for reading the cases selectively.

INDUSTRIAL PRODUCTS DIVISION, MERRIMAC CORPORATION[1]

The case of Merrimac Corp.'s Industrial Products Division provides an illustration of Zero-Base Planning and Budgeting applied for different purposes within one company. The division consisted of three distinct business groups: Plastics, Machine Tools, and Powder Products. The manager of the division had been in charge only six months when he decided to implement Zero Base. One of his objectives was to gain a better understanding of the organization from the lowest levels on up.

The Plastics group, with annual sales of nearly $100 million and an overhead budget of $15 million, engaged in the manufacture and marketing of industrial plastics. Increased competition and the recent emergence of cheaper, synthetic substitutes placed the Plastics group in a position of low growth and declining market share. As a result of the Zero-Base implementation, the Plastics group experienced considerable

---

[1] Names and products of this *Fortune's* top 50 company have been changed.

reallocation. The detailed results are shown in the full case. The overall $15 million Plastics group overhead budget was reduced by over 8 percent.[2]

The Machine Tools group had reduced its staff by ten people during the first half of 1976. Yet, after the final ranking was completed, the group's overhead budget was still further reduced by 4 percent.[3]

The Powder Products group was anticipating rapid growth; consequently, the group's management regarded Zero Base as a means for justifying significant overhead budget increases. They asked for, and received, a budget increase of 50 percent. The division manager commented that: "Without a structured presentation, I would never have approved a budget increase of such magnitude."

UTILITY COMPANY[4]

The second case, Utility Company, concentrates on the use of Zero-Base Planning and Budgeting as a tool to reallocate resources in a functionally organized company; e.g., engineering, marketing, customer services. A thorough account of the problems encountered in this implementation is given. The company had 1975 operating revenues of $137.7 million and expenses of $89.7 million. Management was hopeful that the information obtained through the Zero-Base approach would enable them to make the trade-off between the short-term need to reduce costs and the longer term development of new services and technology.

Utility Company's status as a regulated utility made this implementation unique—in terms of coping with the external forces and in its effect of creating a condition where a number of managers felt no incentive to adopt newer management techniques.

The implementation failed in one sense—no ranking took place at the corporate level. The lack of companywide ranking prevented feedback to the lower level decision unit and ranking managers which would have institutionalized the process. However, middle- and lower level managers did increase their understanding of their operations and improved their decision-making skills.

HEAVY EQUIPMENT DIVISION, LINDEMA CORPORATION[5]

The third case, Heavy Equipment Division, Lindema Corporation, is an examination of the application of Zero Base to a heavy equipment manufacturing company with an $85 million overhead budget. The company was faced with a downturn in business and needed an effective approach to cutting costs and communicating the need for cost control to the organization. Through use of the Zero-Base process, the company did meet the cost-cutting objective, effecting an overall 25 percent overhead reduction in one year.

[2] In real (inflation-adjusted) terms.
[3] Ibid.
[4] This case is a composite of the authors' experiences with utilities.
[5] The name is disguised at the request of the divisional management of this multibillion dollar company.

This case also illustrates many of the problems encountered in implementing Zero-Base Planning and Budgeting in a large, multiplant organization. Many of the difficulties in one plant paralleled another, but the ranking process tended to reflect differing management styles of the plants.

The implementation in the largest department in the company, Engineering, is fully reviewed in this case.

OTTAWA AREA DIVISION OF CANADIAN BROADCASTING CORPORATION

Ottawa Area, a division of the Canadian Broadcasting Corporation, provides the fourth case. This case illustrates the application of Zero-Base Planning and Budgeting to an organization in need of an improved and consistent approach to management planning.

Ottawa Area maintains four radio stations: AM-English; AM-French; FM-English; and FM-French. The division also includes two television stations, one for each language. While a variety of network and local programming is presented to the public, local programming emphasis is on news and current affairs.

A new director, Gordon Bruce, suspected that a significant reallocation of funds was probably needed, but it was unlikely to be effected through the traditional budgeting system. Thus, he selected the Zero-Base approach.

The implementation, which had to be adjusted around the large role that unions play throughout the Canadian Broadcasting Corporation, did achieve a reallocation that pleased Gordon Bruce. He commented: "Our managers are more budget-conscious now, and they possess a greater awareness of their operations." Ottawa Area entered its second Zero-Base Planning and Budgeting cycle in the spring of 1976, with considerably less analytical effort required by various management levels.

ALLIED VAN LINES

In the case of Allied Van Lines, the Zero-Base Planning and Budgeting experience of a large international moving and storage company is related. Allied, a company beset with profit problems, elected to implement the process at the direction of a new president who wanted to learn more about the organization as well as to reduce the budget.

Until 1969, Allied was structured as a nonprofit organization which largely serviced agents. In May 1969, the business charter was changed to create a standard business organization.

Despite the radical change in charter, the performance from 1969 to 1975 was undistinguished. Sales grew rapidly, but profits did not because management was unable to control overhead costs.

Of special interest in this case is the way the final ranking table was drawn—to provide flexibility and to permit effective contingency planning in a business that is both seasonal and cyclical.

The sixth case, GenRad, Inc., is different—it is a teaching case. After having read up to this point, the reader may put himself in the shoes of GenRad management and make decisions about how he would apply Zero Base.

MATRIX

The accompanying matrix will help the reader focus on the characteristics or issues in the various cases that are relevant to his organization or needs.

Background

Of the five industry cases which are indexed in this chapter, two are manufacturers (Merrimac Corp. and Heavy Equipment Division, Lindema Corporation); three are engaged in service (Ottawa Area, Allied Van Lines, Utility Company). The portion of the budgets to which Zero Base applied ranged from a low of 15 percent (as a percentage of sales) in the Plastics group of Merrimac—to 100 percent in the case of Allied.

The growth status of the companies ranged from declining to rapid. The three groups of Merrimac, for instance, were each in a different growth phase and the Zero-Base system was designed for each group's needs. Heavy Equipment Division, Lindema Corporation was facing a 33⅓ percent sales decline. Ottawa Area and Allied expected revenues to grow relatively rapidly. Utility Company expected pressure on growth, but a rate case added uncertainty to their projections.

Objectives

An analysis of the cases presented shows that the companies that devoted a concerted effort to the design—and to introducing it thoroughly—achieved most of their objectives.

Heavy Equipment Division, Lindema Corporation, which faced serious profit pressures following the oil embargo and resulting retrenchments in new apparatus purchases by utilities, and one group of Merrimac, Inc., which wanted a 20 percent overhead reduction, faced critical cost reduction problems. The other companies in the cases did not. Most chose to use Zero-Base Planning and Budgeting as a way to gain control of their overhead expenses. The Powder Products group of Merrimac had the objective of increasing costs significantly through Zero Base.

All of the companies cited in the cases began with a standard cost center reporting system and varied considerably with respect to the level of sophistication of their planning system. For many, the Zero-Base implementation was the first formal planning effort at the lower management level. In all cases, top management viewed the process as a way to improve the analysis skills in lower levels of management. The emphasis of Ottawa Area was especially heavy on improving communication and analysis rather than on cost control.

MATRIX OF CASES

Subject	Industrial Products Division, Merrimac Corporation*			Utility Company*	Heavy Equipment Division, Lindema Corporation*	Ottawa Area	Allied Van Lines
Case	Machine tools	Plastics	Powder products				
1. General background							
Sales	$20 million.	$100 million.	$12 million.	$137.7 million operating budget.	$400 million.	$12.7 million operating budget.	$17.7 million operating budget.
Overhead budget	$4.4 million.	$15 million.	$2.2 million.	$89.7 million.	$85 million.	ZBB applied to $5 million.	ZBB applied to total budget.
Business	Machine tools.	Plastics.	Powder products.	Utility.	Heavy equipment.	TV and radio broadcasting.	International moving and storage.
Current budgeting sophistication	Standard cost center reports.			Managers unsophisticated.	Standard cost center.	Managers had little to do with budget planning.	Standard cost center—low involvement of managers in planning and budgeting.
Profits, trends, environment	Steady.	Mature.	Growing rapidly.	Emerging competition from private firms. Decline in business level.	Business decline—energy crunch.	Business growing slightly.	10% volume increase expected. Seasonal and cyclical business.
2. Objectives	Hold overhead constant. New executive—learn organization. Reallocation of resources. Improve communications. Improve managers' planning abilities. Alternative method of operation.	20% reduction in overhead.	Significant cost increase.	Reduce overhead in selected areas. Justify rate increase and additional overhead spending. Identify active "corporate systems" in a predominantly functional organization. Engineering Department—need for systems-thinking, balanced budget, provision for future.	Dramatic overhead reduction. Create needed data base for reallocation decisions. Alternative methods. Design performance measurements. Improve managers' analytical skills.	Reallocation to high priority areas. Identify nonessential activities being funded. Improve managers' analytical skills. New executive—learn organization. Alternative methods. Develop better planning system.	Overhead cost control. New executive—learn organization. Systematic examination of base of spending. Improve management skills at all levels.
3. Problems during implementation	Defensiveness at plants.			Management at all levels reluctant to make decisions. Difficulty accepting that service levels could vary. Quality of decision unit analyses varied greatly. Lack of visible support from top management. Planning assumptions constantly changing. Disparate expectations for process.	Top management unwilling to devote time to prepare for ranking. "Old-line" ranking manager unresponsive. Engineering Department defensive.	Initial lack of commitment by decision unit managers. Case of "games playing" in ranking. Complacency in Engineering Department. Role of unions.	Lack of preparation by some ranking managers. Ranking of discretionary, yet high potential programs. Managers inexperienced at budgeting and planning.
4. Results	Overhead budget reduction. Improved budgeting-planning relationship. Improved communications. Executive—better understanding of organization.	$200,000 reduction in overhead by using warehouse alternative. Considerable reallocation.	Overhead budget increased 50%.	Increased understanding of departmental operations. Improved budget linkage with long-range plans. Delayed ranking.	Issues raised in process: Centralization, Record-keeping systems, Definition of responsibility. Improved planning assumptions developed. Alternatives few. 25% overhead reduction in one year.	Managers felt ZBB good way to communicate to top. Managers became more budget conscious. Company felt it achieved improved allocation of funds.	Identified and corrected duplication of functions. Performance measurement system improved. Reallocation of funds to new divisions and projects. Managers trained in planning. Ranking provided flexibility in dealing with seasonal and/or cyclical variances.

*Company names have been changed.

Other objectives held in common were: systematic review of the total business—in three of the cases a new chief executive was involved; the opportunity to establish communication between various levels of management about the others' needs and goals. The utility had two unique objectives: justification of a rate increase and identification of corporate systems within a predominantly functional organization. An explicit objective of Utility Company—instilling "systems-thinking" in the Engineering Department—was implicit in Heavy Equipment Division, Lindema Corporation and Ottawa Area.

Problems

Zero-Base Planning and Budgeting problems are most often generated from two sources: (1) the implementation design and (2) that the concept is often perceived as threatening by various levels of management. The cases bear out the second generalization. Defensiveness of managers who perceived the process as a threat or a waste of time came up in virtually every case with the exception of the Plastics group of Merrimac—and there the absence of defensiveness was noteworthy. Approaches which may be used to prevent defensiveness are discussed in Chapter 5.

Other "human" problems are reviewed in addition to defensiveness. Commitment to the Zero-Base process was not always firm. The Lindema, Ottawa, Allied, and Utility cases report lack of commitment at various levels of management. That lack of commitment was sometimes expressed by unpreparedness for certain steps—notably ranking—and also by nonsupportive attitudes. Other problems surfaced: "games-playing" (attempting to push through a pet project by manipulation of the ranking process) in Ottawa; managerial reluctance to make decisions; difficulty accepting variable levels of service; and disparate expectations for the process—as expressed in the Utility Company case.

Accounts of working with all levels of managers in the area of engineering are presented at some length in Lindema, Ottawa, and Utility cases. A usual goal (and resulting difficulty) was the attempt to shift engineers from their traditional, narrow functional approach to recognizing the nature of the functional contribution to the corporate or departmental whole.

Another issue that came up in the Utility Company and Allied Van Lines cases was a variance in the quality of the decision units that were prepared. A disparity such as that can make further analysis less realistic and unreliable. The director of Ottawa Area minimized the disparity difficulty by indicating to the decision unit managers that he would personally review each analysis critically and would, in fact, build the upcoming year's plan on the basis of the analyses. The lower level managers were thus assured that their task was important and that the organization was committed to it.

In Heavy Equipment Division, Lindema Corporation, however, the number of decision units was so large that top-level review was impossible. The problem there was to devise methods to summarize data for top-level review and still assure lower level managers that their analyses would be given a thorough review by someone in the hierarchy.

Changing planning assumptions during the implementation at Utility Company made decision unit analysis difficult. Business fell off inexplicably and the 1977 forecast was in a constant state of revision. This put many managers in the position of estimating 1977 work loads on their own, thereby precluding a uniform approach. The varying forecast also affected projected capital spending, the level of which served as perceived work load for many managers. Imprecise work load projections were less troublesome, however, when the accompanying assumptions were clearly spelled out.

A major problem during the Ottawa Area implementation was the large role that unions play throughout the Canadian Broadcasting Corporation. "Union constraints" was cited as an inhibiting factor many times in the early stages of the implementation. It turned out that the union excuse was overplayed, however. One manager commented: "It is very easy to blame the union for all our troubles, but that is neither practical nor realistic. We need new ideas—the 'union problem' can be reckoned with."

Results

All the companies represented in the cases did not experience overhead reductions. Lindema Corporation effected the greatest reduction—25 percent overall—which was due in part to a significantly lower business volume in 1976. However, greater control and understanding of overhead costs was a result in all cases. In a number of cases control, rather than reduction, had been the objective. The Plastics group achieved a $200,000 reduction in overhead expenses by using a warehouse alternative identified through the process. The Machine Tools group cut their overhead budget by an unanticipated 4 percent in inflation-adjusted terms.

Reallocation was significant in both the Plastics group and Allied Van Lines. The Plastics reallocation is clearly presented in table form. The Allied Van Lines case also provides a good view of the reallocation potential of Zero-Base Planning and Budgeting. The Zero-Base approach resulted in a total budget approximately 10 percent higher than the previous year's budget. The increase was due to the funding of discretionary projects which would enable Allied to meet its profit goals. Identification of the high payoff opportunities and their subsequent funding was an important result for Allied.

The overhead budget increase of 50 percent in the Powder Products group is especially noteworthy. The group management felt confident that their revenue projections justified a budget increase of that magnitude, and met top management's request for detailed justification in the following manner: the ranking table was divided into three strata—maintain, develop, and aggressive growth. Several group meetings were held in which the marketing manager provided future revenue projections and the manufacturing manager projected production capabilities at the various levels.

Group management then met with the division head and presented their revenue plan associated with their proposed overhead budget. Subsequently the total increase was granted by the division head.

Several other results were achieved by Allied. The company was able to identify and correct duplication of functions; and the ranking table was designed to provide flexibility and to permit effective contingency planning for their seasonal and cyclical business.

All companies represented in these cases agreed that the Zero-Base process improved the linkage of various elements of the planning-budgeting systems. The participation of lower level managers in the process increased their understanding of that linkage and their analytical skills, as well. "Improved communication" was cited in a number of cases as a direct result. It was implicit in others where managers, trained in planning through the process, perceived their role in the total scope of the organization for the first time.

5

Problems of implementation

The implementation of a Zero-Base Planning and Budgeting system in an organization can present a steady stream of problems. The purpose of this chapter is to discuss the most frequently encountered problems and give their resolution, based on the experiences of the authors.

This chapter is organized according to the six-step sequence of the process that appears in Chapter 2. An extended preface to the six steps will focus thoroughly on some predictable behavioral reactions and outline methods for administering the process. Familiarity with these areas should help the reader understand how many problems can be avoided—or met and resolved—before the implementation actually begins.

The importance of using a disciplined approach to implementing Zero-Base Planning and Budgeting is paramount. Without sound project planning and management, the process suffers both with respect to the impact on individual managers and to the overall process results.

HUMAN BEHAVIOR ASPECTS

Any new management system provokes some negative response. There may be doubt whether the system is, in fact, "new" or merely the same old system with modifications and a different name. Even if the system is accepted as being new, doubt about top management's commitment to the system may persist.

The introduction of Zero-Base Planning and Budgeting to an organization brings with it the general problems mentioned above and several other ones that apply particularly to this system.

The mere mention of the word "zero" frightens some people. However, the problem of most substance inherent to the Zero-Base process is that it requires management to view the organization in a completely different way. In typical budgeting procedures, an organization's current status is reviewed and then modified upward or downward if a change seems warranted. With Zero Base, however, the organization is perceived as though it were starting anew. Consequently, more opportunity for creativity exists, but more planning is required. With Zero Base, no budget item can be taken for granted.

It is not surprising then, that initial reactions to Zero-Base Planning and Budgeting often include defensiveness and complacency. Before introducing the process effectively, these reactions must be tempered. Part of this discussion will be devoted to a description of how these reactions surface, and how to deal with the problems when they do.

PRE-IMPLEMENTATION PREPARATION FOR DECISION UNIT MANAGERS

Without honest commitment from the decision unit managers, successful implementation of Zero-Base Planning and Budgeting is impossible. Experience has shown that there are three obstacles that must be overcome if the necessary commitment is to be acquired:

1. Decision unit managers feel that their company is different from other companies. Therefore they claim, even if Zero-Base Planning and Budgeting works at other companies, it will not work within their organization.

2. Decision unit managers perceive Zero-Base Planning and Budgeting to be a mere exercise, and that their efforts are irrelevant. They claim that top management is not committed to the process, so why should they care.

3. Decision unit managers neither understand the purpose nor the mechanics of the process. Their reaction, consequently, is defensive.

To overcome the three obstacles mentioned above, the following action steps are recommended:

1. The Zero-Base Planning and Budgeting process must be individually designed for each organization. The manager who says, "A canned approach will not work here" is right! The organization's structure and culture, and other planning and reporting processes must be studied before the appropriate system is designed.

2. The initial communication about Zero Base must be well conceived. The chief executive should prepare a brief memorandum explaining why Zero-Base Planning and Budgeting is being undertaken and what benefits the organization expects to achieve. When Zero Base is first introduced to the decision unit managers, they should be told that this system provides them with a forum to discuss problems, opportunities, and alternatives. Some of the aspects of Zero-Base Planning and Budgeting that should be conveyed to a decision unit manager when he first learns of the process are:

a. This is a communications mechanism by which he can tell his boss how he feels his decision unit should operate. In the past he lacked a channel for expressing his ideas about new and better ways to operate. But now he has a structured forum for presenting new thoughts to top management. In essence, the decision unit manager has a pipeline up the organization.

b. This is also a planning process by which he can show how he would like to build up his department while justifying the desired structure at the same time. A thorough analysis on his part will prevent top management from making "seat of the pants" decisions that could thwart his department's efforts.

After the initial communication a group meeting with decision unit managers and the chief executive should be arranged. The meeting should be devoted to describing the process, detailing responsibilities, outlining benefits, and answering questions. Examples of successful Zero-Base implementations should be presented. In addition, a manual detailing the process and how it works should be provided to each decision unit manager.

3. Since Zero-Base Planning and Budgeting is a new discipline, it is imperative that managers be trained in the process. Although the initial group meeting provides managers with a sound understanding of the concept, individual assistance is recommended throughout the process to ensure appropriate implementation.

ADMINISTRATION OF THE PROCESS

Although each level of management has specific responsibilities during the Zero-Base implementation, there are certain tasks that fall within no one's bailiwick. These tasks include:

1. Establishment of a workplan and timetable for the project.
2. Design of a process that fits the culture of the organization.
3. Preparation of a manual that describes the process to participants in simple, straightforward terms.
4. Delivery of a training presentation to introduce decision unit managers to the process.
5. Assistance to decision unit managers and their superiors with analyses and rankings.

It is probably not possible to administer the process effectively without setting up a task force that spends considerable time on the project. The task force should report to the chief executive officer and should consist of individuals who are familiar with Zero-Base Planning and Budgeting. Others on the task force should be conversant with the organization's financial procedures. The task force often allocates about one person-day of effort per each decision unit manager. This time is usually spent in one-to-two-hour time blocks.

It is important that task force members: (1) possess the required interviewing skills and analytical abilities to apply the process successfully; and (2) be perceived as being objective so that decision unit managers will tend to be candid and open-minded in their analyses; (3) know how to tailor the system to a firm's specific needs.

PROBLEMS OUTLINED IN SIX-STEP FRAMEWORK

Figure 5-1 outlines the steps in the process. Discussion of problem areas will be presented step by step.

FIGURE 5-1
Management involvement in six steps

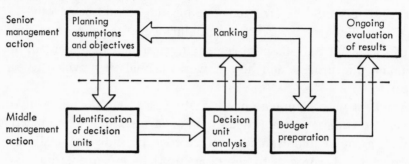

Step 1. Business planning assumptions and budgeting objectives—linkage to Zero-Base process results

Invariably, company plans are developed which stop short of analyzing the implications for the group of management selected as the decision unit level. The reasons are manifold. Typically, a company has a fairly refined view of the general direction that its business is taking and the market and organizational pressures acting on the overall firm. But the initial efforts to analyze decision units reveal that, even though projected rates and profits are well defined, decision unit managers are hard-pressed to envision what specific demands might be made for their services during an upcoming budget cycle. In short, an increasing level of sales means little, taken by itself, to the insurance, personnel, or engineering departments. Most organizations do not link strongly the formal planning system outputs with the implication for individual decision units. As a result of this loose planning/budgeting interrelationship, individual decision unit managers are prone to rely on history to determine the expected demand for their services on which their analyses are to be based, and this in turn leads to some problems.

For example, in a company facing the need for serious cost reduction with the expected result that people will be laid off, the eventual work load expectations for the personnel department will be of increased demand for service in spite of a business decline. Prior to undertaking Zero Base, the issue might be recognized—but in an "across-the-board" movement to be "fair" to all, the issue is subordinated.

Obtaining insight prior to decision unit preparation is a needed prerequisite to realistic analysis. Even as simple an effort as is illustrated in Figure 5-2 will contribute to decision unit manager understanding.

FIGURE 5-2
Expected service trends

Department	Expected service trend for next year	Why
Engineering	↗	New products needed.
Personnel	↗	Must reduce staff levels.
Insurance	→	No change.
Contracts	↘	Decline in number of contracts expected.
Purchasing	↗	Must "professionalize" efforts.

Step 2. Decision unit identification

While the actual selection of decision units at most organizations requires little time, the effects of this selection will be felt throughout implementation of the process. The selection of appropriate decision units is often inhibited by three potential problems: (a) size; (b) ability to make decisions; and (c) time.

a. Decision units are sometimes so small that trade-offs are impractical. For example, if a decision unit with a staff of one person is selected, the options open to management are rather limited.

Conversely, decision units are sometimes so large that a detailed analysis of the various functions is prevented. For example, a 45-person financial staff can be analyzed less effectively as a whole than if it were broken down into more manageable subcomponents such as Accounts Receivable, EDP, and so forth. Hence, a cost center may be comprised of several decision units.

Sometimes decision units are selected such that fractional portions of people are identified for addition or elimination. Such a selection should be discouraged because it limits management's ability to make practical cost/benefit trade-offs.

b. A problem arises if genuine decision units are compared with decision units in which the ability to make decisions is constrained.

c. Any undertaking is limited in what can be accomplished in the time available. Time may become the limiting factor in determining the organizational level at which decision units are prepared.

Step 3. Decision unit analysis—The foundation of the end result

As with any system, the result of using the process is highly dependent on the quality of the input data. The data base in the Zero-Base approach consists mainly of the individual decision unit analyses as they are prepared by decision unit managers. In the situations where new approaches to old problems, or serious cost reduction is the main objective, it is both desirable and beneficial to provide managers with sounding boards for their ideas and challenges to their current opinions and perspectives. This cannot be achieved solely via written instruction or manual writing. It should be supplemented with Zero-Base project personnel meetings with each manager periodically to review analytical efforts, to ask pertinent questions, and to discuss alternative ideas.

These Zero-Base team/decision unit manager meetings generally follow a pattern of four distinct phases of effort:

A. Initial meetings. Initial meetings with the decision unit managers revolve around general topics of organization, purpose, activities, resources, and the historical basis for the decision unit. Decision unit managers tend to ask about the process in several key areas. They want to know about the ranking procedure and how that discussion should be conducted; what quality standards have been set up for decision unit managers; and about the mechanical preparation steps.

In general these initial meetings serve to develop rapport between a decision unit manager and his Zero-Base team assistant. The meetings generally conclude with an assignment suggested by the Zero-Base team member.

B. Structural phase. By the next meeting a decision unit manager is able to cite his objectives, resources, and probable performance measures. Discussions generally focus on the relationship between written statements and the degree to which they reflect the "reality" of the responsibilities in the area.

C. New alternatives phase. During a third get-together, several alternative means of doing the job are discussed. Frequently the discussions center on a history of past ideas which have been considered and rejected. In only about 5 percent of the cases are new alternatives suggested which seem reasonable and attractive. That there are so few new ideas is found to be a function of: settled organizations where functions have "evolved" into their present mode for good reasons; a lack of broad perspective on the part of the decision unit manager who can see options and alternatives only in his own area of responsibility.

However, a Zero-Base team member, working simultaneously with several decision unit managers, can sometimes add up several cross-organizational factors into a reasonable alternative for the overall group, which is then debated during the ranking meeting.

D. Restructuring phase. The fourth and final discussion phase most frequently involves a deliberate, detailed discussion on the incrementalization of the decision unit once the alternative has been chosen.

As a matter of practice, all elements of the eventual analysis are discussed at every meeting with primary emphasis on the current phase of preparation. In this way the decision unit manager continually reinforces his understanding of the objectives of the analysis and the validity of his thinking.

Of particular note in most discussions is the difficulty of defining a true "minimum" increment.

Minimum increment–Key to reallocation potential

There are several reasons why managers have difficulty in defining a minimum increment for his decision unit. First of all, the concept of a minimum increment is difficult to think about since it appears to be a demand for "the same with less." Actually, what is being asked for is a different job than that currently being performed. The manager must focus on structural changes to the job in addition to contractions of effort to achieve the minimum. Most managers start with the notion that they are already at their minimum. It takes a certain amount of discussion with the Zero-Base team member to explain this concept.

A second difficulty in identifying minimum increments is the unwillingness of some decision unit managers to admit that there is a lower level of effort in their general responsibility area that would suffice in a demanding situation. They sense, and correctly so, that identifying a lower level may open them up to a potential reduction of budget. This concern can be overcome to the extent that the overall system is understood and perceived as providing the manager with a fair chance to argue for, and win, his case during the ranking meeting.

A third problem often experienced by managers is the need to prioritize their activities within the decision unit's scope. At first managers tend to take an approach which is illustrated graphically as follows:

ACTIVITY 1
ACTIVITY 2   Minimum increment

ACTIVITY 3   Additional increments

In other words, they see the approach to incrementalization as sequential in nature, requiring that one single activity be fully provided for prior to the inclusion of the next. Eventually, however, the concept of variable service levels of effort within each activity that is needed to accomplish the purpose of the decision unit is understood. The decision unit managers then can organize their increments to include all necessary activities, albeit at variable levels of effort as follows:

Activity 1   Activity 2   Activity 3

Minimum
increment

Additional
increments

This approach acknowledges the "partial, but sufficient" concept that is fundamental to Zero-Base Planning and Budgeting.

The success of the overall Zero-Base process hinges on the development of minimum increments to a large extent. Obviously, if every minimum increment involved 100 percent of the previous year's budget, there would be no way to arrange these increments in the ranking process so that the overall budget could be reduced. In effect putting all of the preexisting decision units "into business" by the acceptance of each minimum increment would involve accepting 100 percent of the previous year's budget regardless of the relative positioning of these increments.

To achieve reallocation requires that true minimums be designated, and to the extent that there are a number of increments in each decision unit between the minimum level and the current level of spending, there is an inherent flexibility to achieve reallocation by prioritization of the increments.

Organizations sometimes make use of "target" percentages to facilitate the individual manager's efforts to define the minimum. A number like 60 percent or 75 percent of the previous year's budget can be chosen to serve as a target goal for each manager. In some areas this is too high a figure, and in others too low, so emphasis remains on finding the true minimum, below which the service level would be so reduced as to make the decision unit ineffectual. In cases where managers come up with minimum increments that exceed the target, a special effort is made to assist the manager in analyzing his decision unit requirements. In this way, the target serves to create an "exception" system so that special analytical effort can be devoted to the areas most in need of it.

The development of acceptable minimum increments depends, in addition to the analytical skill of the decision unit manager, on the degree to which ranking management and/or Zero-Base project team members can ask penetrating questions, and in that way encourage managers to take a hard look at their operations.

Work load and performance measurements

When a decision unit manager is asked to explain what would occur if his budget were decreased substantially, he usually responds by saying *less* work will be performed, *more* complaints from customers will be received, and so on. If he were asked what would occur if his budget were increased substantially, he would say *more* work could be performed, *less* complaints from customers would be received, and so on.

While responses like these may be typical, they are not very helpful to management when decisions relating to budget revisions are needed. Does *more* work mean 2 percent more or 20 percent more? When management considers adding a new man to a decision unit, they want to know the expected return. The problems associated with work load and performance measurements when Zero-Base Planning and Budgeting is implemented are generally of three types: no such measurements have ever been established; very little quantitative data is readily available; the function that these measurements serve is often not understood.

To establish viable work load and performance measurements, the manager must isolate the basic functions carried out by his decision unit. He then must quantify the current activity level of each of the functions. At this point, he will have established a basic framework which can be used in analyzing proposed budget revisions. For example, if manpower were increased by 10 percent, which functions would improve and how much?

The key to establishing appropriate work load and performance measurements is to get the managers to review decision units in detailed analytical fashion. By doing so, the decision unit manager will have a better understanding of what his operations do accomplish and can accomplish, and top management will be in a better position to evaluate potential budget revisions.

During the first year of Zero-Base implementation it is of prime importance for managers to identify their key work load and performance measurements. If they do not possess the data that these measurements demand, the measurements should be listed anyway with the data spaces remaining blank. In subsequent years, managers will know what kind of data is relevant, and then can begin collecting it.

The importance of determining key work load and performance measurements needs to be stressed to all managers. It should be explained that these measurements provide top management with an effective way of evaluating the various departments' efforts. Also, since determination of these measurements requires decision unit managers to specify the major tasks they want performed and their major objectives, this information serves as a useful communication mechanism with top management.

The paperwork

A frequent complaint relating to the Zero-Base Planning and Budgeting process focuses on the apparent superfluity of paperwork. Decision unit managers complain that there are too many forms to prepare, and their superiors complain that there are too many forms to review.

An effective Zero-Base process is designed so that only relevant forms are used. The importance and need for the completion of these forms is conveyed to decision unit managers by the task force. In addition, the managers are told to keep their answers short and to the point.

As was mentioned in a previous section, the preparation of increment summaries by each decision unit manager can be of assistance to top management when they review the analyses.

Step 4. Ranking—The major product

If decision unit analysis is the foundation of the Zero-Base end result, then ranking is the final structure. No amount of elegant ranking can substitute for thoughtfully prepared analysis; on the other hand, a poorly implemented ranking step can effectively wipe out much of the value of the Zero-Base project.

Ranking is in itself a difficult and sometimes uncomfortable affair. For one thing, a discussion between peers can sometimes reverse the "cherished notions" that senior managers hold about both the substance of their responsibility area and their perception about what their decision unit managers really think about their jobs.

Preparing for ranking

The quality of thought and preparation effort that goes into a decision unit shows up clearly in the ranking process if it is properly conducted. Poor quality is indicated when: managers have difficulty understanding the unit or its implications; the ranking group continually finds itself wanting to send decision units back to the drawing board for restructuring.

Ranking meetings generally succeed in getting the job of prioritization done. Some meetings, however, are characterized by a great deal of difficulty that might have been avoided through the use of more structured approach. Often the difficulties are a result of insufficient preparation by ranking managers.

Ranking managers who come to their meetings without first making an honest effort to understand each decision unit managers' unit, generally conclude that the system is simply a "means for justifying what has been done in the past." This perception comes about because in the absence of shared understanding with each decision unit manager—based upon prior discussion of the analysis—the only bases for meaningful discussion are the "old" conversations and understanding between the decision unit manager and his ranking manager. Obviously, such discussion will entail "what has been done in the past."

Comparing decision units

Since decision units in a given organization may range from "drafting" in the Engineering Department to "receivables" in the Finance Department to "administration" in the Personnel Department, top management occasionally questions whether an equitable comparison of diverse decision units can be performed in a relatively short time frame. Also, they wonder how work load and performance measurements can be of use to them since they differ widely across decision units.

To avoid comparability problems, extreme care must be taken to ensure that the Zero-Base Planning and Budgeting forms are tailored to an organization's particular needs and that all decision unit managers abide by the conventions. The Zero-Base process requires managers to view their decision units analytically, and in a consistent fashion. Therefore, consistent presentation is essential if top management is to compare and rank diverse decision units intelligently.

Although work load and performance measurements differ across decision units, the differences do not prevent equitable comparisons. Appropriate work load and performance measurements allow fair cost/benefit analyses to be made not only within a particular decision unit, but also across increments of different decision units.

It is important to realize, however, that the Zero-Base process depends for its success on face-to-face communication. No set of forms, however elaborate, can possibly contain the whole story and thereby permit armchair decision making. Rather, the forms must serve as an agenda to guide discussions in a balanced way in all the important areas of a decision unit manager's responsibility. As such, the system demands that managers take the time to read the key phrases and sentences on the forms and also to question the preparer to better understand his reasoning and approach.

A typical session

The typical ranking process discussion begins with an educationally oriented discussion with each decision unit manager taking his turn to explain the basic objective of his decision unit and the reasons why he chose that increment structure. Each manager also discusses the consequences and benefits of each increment and its total cost to the organization. After this initial round of questions and answers, the process of ranking begins.

The mechanical aspect of the ranking process in most cases entails taking the minimum increment from each decision unit and placing them side by side on a table or blackboard. The group discussion then focuses on these minimum increments until one is chosen to be first in the ranking table. At this point, the second increment of the selected decision unit is substituted for the first and a new round of discussions proceed. In this way, there are visible to the group only the same number of increments at any one time as there are decision units under consideration, thereby limiting the scope of discussion to a few specific competing increments. Eventually, all increments are examined and the ranking list completed.

With each round of discussion, the criteria by which increments are accepted next into the ranking are discussed and continue to guide increment acceptance. Frequently, these criteria change as increments are incorporated into the list. For example, initial discussion frequently focuses on "survival" level needs and meeting fundamental business and legal needs. As increments are accepted into the ranking, the discussion focuses more on patching up "leaks in the boat" or reinforcing areas of recent interest or importance. Toward the end of the ranking list, criteria shift to the pursuit of excellence, making life more comfortable, or other issues of a discretionary character.

In a representative staff ranking, the criteria shown in Figure 5-3 were recorded in the order of their appearance during the discussion.

FIGURE 5-3
Ranking criteria

Order of appearance	Ranking criteria discussed	
1.	Meeting legal requirements.	
2.	Meeting the operating units' needs.	
3.	Helping senior management decision making.	
4.	Providing for the future as opposed to fire fighting.	"Necessities"
5.	Providing "administrative" necessities.	
6.	Moving toward centralization.	
7.	Meeting contract obligations.	
8.	Meeting legal needs.	
9.	Formulating management policy.	
10.	Centralizing functions.	
11.	Reducing costs.	"Probables"
12.	Preventing problems.	
13.	Meeting management's funding expectations.	
14.	Absorbing some line responsibilities.	
15.	Providing for corporate policy needs.	
16.	Preserving the status quo.	"Possibles"
17.	Increasing control over function.	
18.	Meeting potential funding level.	

One can read through these "reasons" for accepting increments and gain an insight into the relative priorities of the organization. Several criteria recur in the ranking discussion. Some provide for the acceptance of one increment and then disappear from the discussion. Throughout the discussion, there often occurs a balancing act which combines political and interpersonal factors with risk and reward factors in a complex mix to find an acceptable ranking of prioritized increments. At the end of the process, most managers have given up something and gained something and feel as a result, that the process was fair. Moreover, they understand the "reasons why" certain activities and service levels were funded before others.

Top management review

By the time decision unit increments are ready for top management review, the number of increments to be ranked may be several hundred in large organizations. Detailed scrutiny of each increment would require an excessive amount of time. Consequently, top management is faced with a problem of reviewing a lot of information in rapid order.

A process, referred to as the "ABC Approach to Ranking," has proven itself to be effective and fast. This approach requires top management to briefly scan each increment, with the decision unit managers if appropriate, and then to categorize the increments into three basic groups:

A   Those increments that, in top management's opinion, must be funded.
B   Those increments that top management considers to be somewhat discretionary.
C   Those increments that top management believes should not be funded.

After the categorization is completed, top management can spend all their efforts on B rankings. If there are 200 increments to be ranked, it is irrelevant whether an increment is ranked number 3 or number 33 (both are A items and will be funded), and it is irrelevant if an increment is ranked number 166 or 196 (both are C items and will not be funded). The B items will, in essence, comprise the truly rankable increments, or the gray area of the budget that generally covers expenditures that fall roughly between 85 percent and 120 percent of last year's budget.

The "ABC Approach to Ranking" provides management with a systematic procedure that can be applied in a short period of time. Without a systematic method of ranking, good analyses by lower management will often not receive the attention they merit. Whereas top management ranking requires little time relative to the incremental analyses by decision unit managers, the entire Zero-Base Planning and Budgeting process will be implemented unsatisfactorily without a good ranking process.

In addition to the "ABC Approach to Ranking," top management sometimes uses other techniques to cope with the large amount of information in a short period of time. For example, top management occasionally requests each decision unit manager to prepare a simple summary of his incremental analyses. In this manner, top management can become aware of the most important information without sorting through much paperwork.

Top management frequently likes to begin the ranking process by making use of "red flag" analysis. This technique allows top management to compare the changes in expenditure level for a given service level. For example, if it would cost 40 percent more to provide the same level of service as last year for a given decision unit, the "red flag" analysis would highlight this variance.

Gamesmanship

Some decision unit managers have attempted to subvert the Zero-Base system by placing low-priority activities in the minimum increment and key programs and projects in the later increments. These managers reasoned that the later increments would not be approved until the minimum increment was funded, and that the later increments were of prime importance to top management. Consequently, the managers felt they could rig the system to give themselves a larger budget.

The gamesmanship attempts of most managers have been unsuccessful because the incremental analyses require detailed evaluations of each increment. In addition, rankings are reviewed at successive levels of management and are challenged and rearranged by them where appropriate.

Consequently, a detailed scrutiny of the increment order both by peers and by higher management levels provide an effective control against successful "games playing."

If "games playing" were successful, the entire Zero-Base Planning and Budgeting process would be worthless. This presents a strong case for ensuring that the process is implemented appropriately. Some people deduce that once the Zero-Base Planning and Budgeting concept is understood, it can be readily applied. This assumption has led firms that have attempted Zero-Base implementation and failed, to conclude that the Zero-Base Planning and Budgeting process cannot work for them. The problem, of course, is not that the process was ineffective, but rather that the implementation was inadequate.

Step 5. Budget preparation

The end product of an implementation is a priority-related ranking table incorporating all decision unit increments. There will be a cumulative dollar total on the ranking table above which all increments are funded and below which no increments are funded. The group of funded increments comprise the upcoming year's budget and correspond directly to a budget prepared in the traditional way.

Sometimes organizations using Zero Base for the first time disregard the "tried and true" aspects of auditing budgets. As a result the backup for the increments is sloppy. The line items are not audited and certain expenditures are too high or too low.

The traditional audit of line items should be continued under Zero-Base Planning and Budgeting. It is best to work with decision unit managers after their ranking has been completed and the increments have been approved. Good auditing in the final preparation stage can yield as much as a 2 percent additional reduction in costs. Normally, however, the cost tightening from the audit is much less than 2 percent.

Step 6. Ongoing evaluation of results

Whereas some systematic analyses of overhead activities are designed to be a one-time procedure, Zero-Base Planning and Budgeting is an ongoing management process.

Without appropriate follow-up activity, however, the process will soon become ineffective. Therefore, to institutionalize Zero-Base Planning and Budgeting successfully in any organization, the system needs to be monitored. The problem that some organizations have encountered is determining the appropriate method of follow-up. That method is discussed in Chapter 2.

SUMMARY

Zero-Base Planning and Budgeting has suddenly drawn the focus of managers in both the public and private sector. However, it is a concept that has been on the scene—steadily growing in acceptance—since the early 1970s. That growth has occurred because Zero-Base Planning and Budgeting works. It does provide a reasonable approach to controlling overhead costs and to resource allocation within a firm or agency.

Results from the 75 implementations that have been directed by our firm have been impressive. Budget reductions have been accomplished; the process has enabled management to learn how overhead costs are generated; and that information has been developed in a way that management can trade off to achieve maximum utilization of resources.

As the results of some of the most recent implementations are analyzed, high marks have been given to areas that originally were considered by-products of the process. The participation of lower-level managers has, in a number of instances, meant that they perceived their role in the total scope of the organization for the first time. Communication between various levels of management has, in fact, been improved through implementations of the process.

It can't be stated too strongly that care must be exercised in designing an implementation for a specific organization to accommodate individual cultural or environmental characteristics. When that care is taken, Zero-Base Planning and Budgeting is indeed, an excellent management tool.

appendix

Merrimac Corporation*

Robert Sandton had been manager at the corporation's Industrial Products Division for only six months when he decided to implement Zero-Base Planning and Budgeting within his organization. The Industrial Products Division consisted of three distinct business groups: Plastics, Machine Tools, and Powder Products.

The Plastics group, with annual sales of nearly $100 million and an overhead budget of $15 million, engaged in the manufacture and marketing of industrial plastics. Increased competition and the recent emergence of cheaper, synthetic substitutes placed the Plastics group in a position of low growth and declining market share.

The Machine Tools group, with annual sales of nearly $20 million, and an overhead budget of $4.4 million, manufactured and marketed industrial strap and strapping equipment. This business group was growing moderately.

The Powder Products group, with annual sales of $12 million, and an overhead budget of $2.2 million, engaged in the manufacture and marketing of patented powder-like substances that the pharmaceutical and food industries aggressively sought. This business group was growing rapidly.

OBJECTIVES

As a new division head, Sandton had several objectives in mind when he decided to implement Zero-Base Planning and Budgeting for his organization. These objectives were: (1) reallocation of resources among the three business groups; (2) improved communication among managers within each business group; (3) training in the disciplines of planning and budgeting for inexperienced and lower level managers; and (4) a better understanding personally, of his organization from the lowest levels on up.

The 1977 sales forecast dictated that the Plastics group substantially reduce overhead expense; the Machine Tools group remain at a comparable overhead level with 1976; and the Powder Products group expand significantly. Rather than rely on arbitrary across-the-board changes, Sandton preferred the idea of a decision unit by decision unit analysis.

*The corporate, divisional, and group names have been disguised. The name of the divisional manager is also fictitious.

IMPLEMENTATION—PLASTICS GROUP

Since it was implicitly assumed that expense reductions would occur in the Plastics group, a defensive reaction from some of the decision unit managers was anticipated. However, little defensiveness surfaced. This was partly due to general management's very positive presentation of Zero Base to lower level managers. Most managers approached the process with enthusiasm and candor. For example, when one of the regional sales managers was asked what his reaction would be if his sales force were reduced from nine to seven salesmen, he said he would welcome it. He felt that such a reduction would provide the remaining salesmen with larger territories, greater potential sales revenue, and consequently, enhanced motivation.

Decision unit analyses provided a means for identifying and evaluating some significant alternative operating modes. For example, the distribution manager suggested that one of the major regional distribution centers discontinue on-site customer specification slitting and rent public facility warehouse space instead. After reviewing the data, Sandton concurred with the suggestion and it resulted in an annual overhead expense reduction of $200,000.

In the final ranking of the Plastics group, Sandton achieved a considerable reallocation. The Marketing Department's overhead expense was reduced by 20 percent in real (inflation-adjusted) terms as the group's marketing strategy was further geared toward a mature mode of operations. However, the Manufacturing plant's overhead expense was increased by 5 percent in real terms to continue maintenance activities.

Table 1 shows clearly the reallocation which resulted from implementation of Zero-Base Planning and Budgeting. The $15 million Plastics group overhead budget

TABLE 1
Reallocation in Plastics group

Decision unit	Expense change (inflation-adjusted) (percent)	Staff change (percent)	Notes
Central Region sales	(8%)	—	No change.
Western Region sales	(22)	(22.2%)	Eliminate 1 salesman; eliminate 1 office clerk.
Southeast Region sales	(16)	(21.4)	Eliminate 2 salesmen; eliminate 1 office clerk.
Northeast Region sales	(25)	(27.8)	Eliminate 3 salesmen; eliminate 1 office manager; eliminate 1 secretary.
Southwest Region sales	(9)	(14.3)	Eliminate 1 office clerk.
International sales	(25)	—	Reduced agent commissions.
Administration	3	—	No change.
Marketing services	(33)	(33.3)	Eliminate 1 market manager.
Advertising and publicity staffing	(40)	(33.3)	Eliminate 1 publicity manager.
Advertising and promotion programs . .	(52)	—	Reduced advertising programs.
Marketing—Subtotal	(20)	(14.4)	
West Coast distribution	(8)	—	No change.
Midwest distribution	(72)	(90.0)	Use public warehouse—no slitting.
Southeast distribution	(74)	(100.0)	Use public warehouse—no slitting.
Southwest distribution	(79)	(100.0)	Use public warehouse—no slitting.
Administration—distribution	(13)	—	No change.
Distribution—Subtotal	(51)	(58.8)	

TABLE 1 (continued)

Decision unit	Expense change (inflation-adjusted) (percent)	Staff change (percent)	Notes
Field service and converter activity—technical service	(3%)	(11.1%)	Eliminate 1 international technical service representative.
Product service—technical service	(34)	(30.0)	Eliminate 1 technical service representative; eliminate 1 technician; eliminate 1 secretary.
Management—technical service	(15)	(50.0)	Eliminate 1 secretary.
Technical—Subtotal	(12)	(23.8)	
R.&D., Plant 1	(3)	—	No change.
R.&D., Plant 2	(30)	(38.5)	Eliminate 1 process engineer; eliminate 1 senior research chemist; eliminate 3 technicians.
R.&D. administration	(20)	(16.7)	Use FDA coordinator on part-time basis only.
R.&D.—Subtotal	(22)	(25.0)	
Plant management—Plant 1	3	7.7	Add 1 operations manager.
Engineering administrator—Plant 1	—	—	No change.
Employee relations—Plant 1	(25)	(9.1)	Eliminate 1 supervisor of employee services.
Technical control—Lab. 4—Plant 1	—	—	No change.
Technical control—Lab. 3—Plant 1	—	—	No change.
Process control—Plant 1	—	—	No change.
Quality control—Plant 1	—	—	No change.
Process and factory improvement—Plant 1	86	75.0	Add 2 process improvement engineers; add 1 senior technician.
Viscose—engineering maintenance—Plant 1	6	—	Increased business and maintenance services.
Spinning—engineering maintenance—Plant 1	2	1.6	Increased maintenance material.
Coating—engineering maintenance—Plant 1	17	0.8	Increased maintenance material.
Finishing—engineering maintenance—Plant 1	(21)	—	Reduced maintenance material.
Utilities—engineering maintenance—Plant 1	7	—	Increased business and maintenance services.
Central shops—engineering maintenance—Plant 1	25	—	Increased business and maintenance services.
Acid reclaim—engineering maintenance—Plant 1	(16)	3.5	Reduced business and maintenance services.
Accounting—Plant 1	4	—	No change.
M.I.S.—Plant 1	—	—	No change.
Stores—Plant 1	—	4.3	Add 1 stores attendant.
Purchasing—Plant 1	—	—	No change.
Plant 1—Subtotal	4	1.5	
Controllers—excluding M.I.S.	(3)	—	Eliminate 1 consolidations accountant by 4/1/77
Controllers—M.I.S.	—	—	No change.
Controller—Subtotal	(3)	—	
Total	(8)	(6.7)	

was reduced by over 8 percent in real terms. When asked to comment on the Zero-Base results, the marketing director, whose department was reduced by 20 percent in real terms, commented that "the cutback in the Marketing area was equitable." The Technical Service Department manager, whose budget was cut by over 12 percent in real terms, stated that "Zero-Base Planning and Budgeting made my people better managers."

The Zero-Base process also raised several issues within the Plastics group that were brought to top management's attention. Among them were the possibility of instituting a centralized order entry system and the design of an effective and equitable incentive system to raise salesman morale and motivation.

IMPLEMENTATION—MACHINE TOOLS

During the first half of 1976, the Machine Tools group had reduced its staff by ten people. Consequently, there was limited anticipation of any further reduction, and it would have seemed logical that manager defensiveness would have been at a minimum. However, at one of the plant locations several managers approached the Zero-Base process with a defensive posture. These managers, it was later realized, perceived themselves as supervisors and felt that planning and budgeting tasks were to be assumed only by the plant manager. By the end of the implementation, the Zero-Base process seemed to change their perception of themselves and to provide them with needed managerial training.

In contrast to the plant managers' defensive reaction, the Marketing department managers received Zero-Base Planning and Budgeting enthusiastically. Since several of these managers had been recently promoted to their positions, they were faced with their first budgeting experience. They considered the Zero-Base process simple and straightforward, and an effective way for them to analyze their newly inherited departments.

The Machine Tools group manager had instructed his decision unit managers and ranking managers to prepare their incremental analyses and rankings in accordance with a three-layer strategic plan. The first represented a bare-bones existence level which he labeled "harvest."

The second layer represented, essentially, status quo which he termed "maintain." The third layer represented expansion of operations and was labeled "maintain and selectively invest." Each stratum included several increments. By structuring his ranking in such a manner, the Machine Tools manager was able to integrate his strategic, intermediate-range plan with his short-term, operating plan. Sandton found this ranking technique illuminating, in terms of determining the 1977 budget.

After the final ranking was completed, the Machine Tools group's overhead budget was reduced by 4 percent in real terms. This reduction was somewhat surprising in view of the fact that the staff level had been reduced by ten persons just prior to the implementation. Yet, the reaction of group management to the reduction was generally favorable. Figures for this group are summarized in Table 2. Although

TABLE 2
Reallocation in Machine Tools group

Decision unit	Expense change (inflation-adjusted) (percent)	Staff change (percent)	Notes
East sales	(4%)	(8.3%)	Eliminate 1 salesman.
Midwest sales	(13)	16.7	Add 1 salesman.
West sales	(2)	—	No change.
Marketing services	(10)	(18.2)	Eliminate 1 administrative manager; eliminate 1 clerk.
Sales administration	12	—	No change.
Advertising	(20)	—	Reduced advertising programs.
Marketing—Subtotal	(5)	(5.7)	
Machinery development	(1)	—	No change.
Equipment development	(31)	(28.6)	Eliminate 2 design engineers.
Research and development— Subtotal	(14)	(11.1)	
Production—Plant 1	(2)	—	No change.
Purchasing—Plant 1	12	—	No change.
Quality and reliability—Plant 1	3	—	No change.
Controller—Plant 1	5	—	No change.
Manufacturing—engineering—Plant 1	(1)	—	No change.
Administration—Plant 1	—	—	No change.
Plant 1—Subtotal	—	—	
Machinery—Plant 2	(18)	(27.3)	Eliminate 1 shift supervisor; eliminate 2 quality control technicians.
Materials—Plant 2	5	—	No change.
Maintenance—Plant 2	(5)	—	No change.
Management—Plant 2	(1)	16.7	Add 1 clerk.
Administration—Plant 2	2	—	No change.
Engineering and technology—Plant 2	3	—	No change.
Plant 2—Subtotal	(3)	(3.4)	
Total	(5)	(4.2)	

moderate reallocation occurred in general, the results were not nearly as dramatic as those in the Plastics group. In the case of the Machine Tools manufacturing plant, no reallocation took place.

IMPLEMENTATION—POWDER PRODUCTS GROUP

In its most recent fiscal year, the Powder Products group had experienced a pretax return on capital employed of 23 percent. Future prospects appeared bright and rapid growth was anticipated. Consequently, Powder Products group management regarded the Zero-Base Planning and Budgeting process as a means for justifying significant overhead budget increases.

After all the decision unit increments were prepared and ranked, the problem facing the group's management was convincing Sandton to grant them a budget that amounted to a real increase of 50 percent over their 1976 level.

Although Sandton was presented with a Powder Products group ranking table, he asked that more information be provided to him before making a funding decision. He requested the Powder Products group management to break their ranking table into three layers, using the technique of the Machine Tools group management. In addition, he wanted to see revenue estimates over the next three years and the impact that the various overhead budget layers would have on these estimates.

The Powder Products group management felt confident that their revenue projections justified a budget increase of 50 percent, and embarked upon the task of meeting Sandton's request. The ranking table layers were identified as follows: maintain; develop; and aggressive growth. Several group meetings were held in which the marketing manager provided future revenue projections and the manufacturing manager projected production capabilities at the various strata.

At their next meeting with Sandton, the group management presented their revenue plan associated with their proposed overhead budget. After evaluating the information carefully, Sandton granted Powder Products group management's total request. See Table 3 for breakdown of changes within the department.

Sandton later said: "Without a structured presentation, I would never have approved a budget increase of such magnitude."

TABLE 3
Reallocation in Powder Products group

Decision unit	Expense change (inflation-adjusted) (percent)	Staff change (percent)	Notes
Manufacturing	45%	28.6%	Add 1 production planner; add 1 manufacturing clerk.
Engineering	64	16.7	Add 1 project manager; add 1 storeroom attendant; more project maintenance.
Technical—Plant	(8)	—	No change.
Plant accounting	37	16.3	More plant managerial accountants.
Marketing	39	18.2	Add 1 market research; add 1 clerk; greater search for new markets.
Plant management	10	5.3	More effective Safety and Employment Relations Program.
Research and development	27	23.5	Add 1 chemical engineer; add 1 product development chemist; add 2 technicians.
Administration	111	57.1	Staff and expense requirement for start-up of Irish plant.
Process improvement	1,062	200.0	Conduct process improvement study.
Total	50	23.6	

CONCLUSION

The implementation of Zero Base Planning and Budgeting at Merrimac's Industrial Products Division resulted in significant reallocations. In addition, as the implementation evolved, it proved to be a meaningful vehicle for integration of short-term and intermediate-range strategic plans.

Although the implementation was deemed successful in general, several managers felt that the process was not particularly effective at the manufacturing plant level. It was felt that few creative alternatives resulted from the implementation and that the plants were already operating at skeletal support staff levels.

Sandton, however, achieved the goals he had set for the process initially:

- Resource reallocation among the three business groups.
- Improved communication among managers.
- Meaningful training for inexperienced managers.
- A better understanding, personally, of the entire organization.

In fact, at the conclusion of the ranking process, Sandton commented: "Not only did the Zero-Base process achieve the objectives I had set for it, but it also took less time and effort than I expected. I will recommend that other corporate divisions implement it."

An evaluation of the implementation at Industrial Products Division that resulted from answers to a questionnaire sent to decision unit managers follows this case.

USERS' EVALUATION OF ZERO BASE[1]

The majority of benefits accrue to top management. The average decision unit manager merely acts as a conduit of information to higher management. Overall the most valuable item is the preparation of a detailed overhead plan.

Upon completion of the Zero-Base Planning and Budgeting exercise, a questionnaire was sent to the decision unit managers. The replies from the questionnaire were relatively consistent between departments. The decision unit managers ranked the following to be the most significant benefits received from the process: (1) identification of activities and costs; (2) more explicit planning by managers; (3) clarification of goals and objectives; and (4) informed decision making.

The next grouping was perceived to be of lesser importance: (1) successful justification of additional requirements; and (2) development of managers.

The following were perceived to be of minor importance: (1) prioritization of activities; (2) communication across division functional lines; (3) education of managers; and (4) communications across plant lines.

In addition to ranking the above benefits the decision unit managers were also asked to comment on the difficulties they had encountered during the process and how valuable the Zero-Base process was to their organization. About 25 percent of the decision unit managers felt that Zero-Base Planning and Budgeting did not impose

[1] This evaluation was received by the consultants following the completion of the Zero-Base process at Industrial Products Division.

any difficulties. The remainder of the decision unit managers encountered the following difficulties:

1. Confusion in the beginning over increments.
2. Work load measures were difficult to generate.
3. The process emphasizes cost cutting only.
4. A greater budget work load.
5. Division objectives were weak.
6. Not enough time.
7. Not integrated into the normal budget process.
8. Forms are too detailed, time consuming, and computations were tedious.
9. Told to do, not sold on.
10. Bad feelings between departments.
11. No ranking input.
12. Examples in manual were poor.

About 9 percent of the decision unit managers felt that Zero-Base Planning and Budgeting was of no value to their organization, and about 5 percent were unsure of its value. The remainder, or 86 percent, felt that the process was of value and highlighted the following areas:

1. Pinpoints areas of responsibility.
2. Greater interdepartment communications.
3. Better understanding of division objectives.
4. Better understanding of business.
5. Good for cost cutting.
6. Justifies activity.
7. Orderly planning and management development tool.
8. Aids in planning.
9. Coordinate functions.
10. Review of individual efforts and objectives.
11. Participation in the budget.
12. Gives higher management a detailed view.
13. Assisted in decision making.

case two

Utility Company *

Utility Company was faced with a myriad of problems unique to its position as a public utility when it turned to Zero-Base Planning and Budgeting as a source of help.

Because the company is a regulated utility, its cost structure is under continuous scrutiny by the Public Utilities Commission, which requests justification and explanation of costs on a regular basis. In addition, the company has had to seek frequent rate increases to attract the capital required to maintain a high level of service to its subscribers.

Utility Company, with 1975 operating revenues of $137.7 million and expenses of $89.7 million, had gone through a series of budget reductions in recent years. Its management believed that the company was at a point where any further expense reduction would impair its ability to manage the $145 million per year of capital expenses needed to maintain service standards. It was felt that further reductions would have virtually eliminated the company's capability to deal with the future in areas of new technology, new service offerings, and management development.

In order to continue to control costs and to bring them in line with decreasing revenue, the company decided to conduct a trial implementation of Zero-Base Planning and Budgeting. The trial indicated that the Zero-Base approach was appropriate for their needs. The information developed would enable them to make the trade-off between the short-term need to reduce costs and the longer-term development of new services and technology.

The company then prepared to implement the process on a company-wide basis through its Corporate Planning Department which had the responsibility for managing and coordinating the budgeting process.

OBJECTIVES

Three objectives were identified for the implementation in addition to the development of the 1977 operating budget. The most important objective in the short term was to isolate the areas in which budget reductions could still be effected and then to assess the potential impact of such reductions.

*This case is a composite of the authors' experiences with utilities.

Secondly, by having all expenses described in cost/benefit/consequence terms, management believed that it would be in a better position to determine an appropriate overall expense level to present to the Public Utilities Commission.

A third objective involved the organization of the company. Top management was accustomed to viewing activities in purely functionally-related terms rather than in the corporate context. Typical of many utilities, Utility Company was functionally organized into four primary groupings:

1. Operating—(a) plant, (b) marketing, (c) facilities, and (d) purchasing.
2. Planning—(a) corporate planning, (b) research, (c) engineering, (d) information services, (3) external affairs, and (f) intercorporate affairs.
3. Finance—(a) financial accounting, (b) financial planning, (c) regulatory affairs, (d) treasury, and (e) management information.
4. Organization development.

Although the functional organization was strongly imbedded, it was generally recognized that there were some strong "corporate systems" running through the organization across functional lines. The most important of these corporate systems were those related to capacity and associated activities.

The third objective, then, was to make certain that functional and corporate system needs were balanced and coordinated.

ENVIRONMENT

A number of environmental conditions posed difficulties during the implementation of Zero-Base Planning and Budgeting.

Existing planning system

The condition, functioning, and acceptance of the existing long-range planning system made it difficult for a decision unit manager to relate his activities to an overall corporate purpose. The problem was amplified during this budget cycle because there was no formal long-range plan issued. In general, planning within the company could be characterized as functionally oriented. Fairly specific goals were formulated by top management and communicated down to middle and lower management. Budgeting, then, meant specifying the resources required to meet the corporate objectives, which in many cases were quite precisely defined.

Culture

A second condition related to the culture of the firm. As is the case in several regulated businesses, some managers felt no incentive to adopt newer management techniques. Some, who felt they had "tenure," did not seem to be motivated to adopt new ways of thinking.

In contrast, a large number of younger, aggressive, analytical managers welcomed improvements in the company's management processes and were willing to provide the critical self-examination required for high-quality Zero-Base analyses. The variance in managers' capabilities and interest resulted in differences in analytical quality which, in turn, affected the ability of higher level managers to make decisions.

IMPLEMENTATION OF THE PROCESS

The implementation of Zero-Base Planning and Budgeting for Utility Co. is described here by the major steps in the process.

Decision unit selection

Decision units corresponded basically to existing budget centers associated with the second level of management. The major exception to this approach was in the Engineering Department. Although the Engineering Department was organized functionally, the chief engineer realized that each of these groups contained activities which were related in an integral—although undefined—way to various processes flowing through the department, such as increasing capacity, increasing service levels, and planning and budgeting. Therefore it was decided to start with existing budget centers and then subdivide them into their component parts. Those parts represented more basic activities focused on purpose rather than function.

At this point it was not possible to create decision units wholly appropriate for a cross-functional analysis for two reasons: (1) the nature and components of the cross-functional flows were not fully defined; and (2) no person could be identified as being responsible for an analysis that would cut across the department.

Decision unit analysis

The primary input into the work load identification came from the Planning Department in the form of the customer requirements forecast, which projected revenues. Unfortunately, over the course of the implementation, actual business volume varied and the 1977 forecast was in a constant state of revision. This put many managers in the position of estimating the 1977 work load on their own, thereby effectively precluding a uniform approach. The varying forecast also affected projected capital spending, the level of which served as perceived work load for many managers.

Capital spending was the buffer used to absorb revenue fluctuations, therefore the uncertain 1977 revenue forecast led to an uncertain 1977 capital spending level—again forcing many managers to make their own volume assumptions. It was felt that an imprecise work load assumption would not present too great a problem as long as the assumptions were clearly spelled out.

The overall quality of the analyses was a direct function of the department manager's interest and participation. The analyses, however, were also affected by factors which were out of the control of the individual department head. Several cases in the Marketing Department serve as an example.

Although the marketing manager was quite receptive to the idea of a new process, there were two immediate problems. The first was gaining the acceptance by lower level managers of the concept that service or quality could be a variable; the second related to the effect of the existing control system on the managers' behavior.

Service standards were typically set by senior management. It was then the responsibility of the decision unit managers to translate their standards into an operating budget using productivity factors. There was a great reluctance on the part of the decision unit managers to propose several levels of service/quality along with the resultant costs. This reluctance stemmed partially from the fact that Utility Company never before consciously decided to offer a lower grade of service to the customer and partially from the belief that the Public Utilities Commission would never let the company downgrade service. Eventually the managers were persuaded that this type of information would be meaningful to top management by allowing them to fully understand the cost of providing a high level of service.

The second problem had the most effect on the quality of the decision unit analyses. Operating under a highly measurement-oriented control system (typical in this industry) led to a condition in which individual managers associated resources—people—with their effect on the measurements rather than with functional activities, the performance of which would improve measurements. Frequently the analyses would state that a resource would be added to "improve Business Office accessibility to 90" or "improve the billing index to 96" rather than to "provide additional capacity in the business office to serve the customer better" or "provide the depth to allow better control over the quality of billing information and hence improve the index." The Zero-Base process encouraged managers to focus on the way the job was being accomplished, that is, the relationship between resources, activities, and measurements, as opposed to only the measurements.

Due to the personal interest and enthusiasm of the department manager and the third-level managers reporting to him, decision unit managers received positive feedback and were able to progressively polish their analyses so that, on balance, they were of above average quality.

RANKING

The ranking process revealed much of the organizational character of the company and displayed the ability of the Zero-Base Planning and Budgeting process to bridge the gap between corporate planning considerations and the construction of a functional departmental operating budget.

Ranking typically began at the third level (i.e., two levels above the decision unit) of management and was necessarily functional in nature with little consideration given to interdepartmental effects. Third-level managers felt that it was important to communicate their "needs" and felt that any interdepartmental imbalance could be rectified during subsequent rankings. In one department, ranking began at the second level of management and made visible, for the first time, a potentially serious management development problem within that department.

An interesting characteristic of each ranking was that ranking managers resisted ranking increments below the current level of operations. Even though Zero-Base Planning and Budgeting was introduced as a decision support system that would allow proactive (as opposed to reactive) decision making, some ranking managers tended to avoid the decision-making requirement of the process. Consequently the ranking process was viewed as a process to generate information (the incremental analysis) to be used when decision making was required.

Another general observation about the ranking process was the relative untouchability of the management structure. Most ranking managers made the conscious decision that at any level of expenditures and services it would not be realistic to assume that the management required to support that service level would be a variable.

Ranking at the department head level was similar to that at the third level of management, with the exception of the Engineering Department. In all cases, however, an important requirement of the Zero-Base process was reinforced—the requirement that the ranking manager make a time and effort commitment to understand the detailed analyses prior to any ranking. The marketing departmental ranking provided a good example.

MARKETING

After spending two to three hours with each of his third-level ranking managers reviewing their rankings and logic in detail, the marketing manager went on vacation, taking with him a binder containing all the decision unit analyses—with the good intention of reviewing each in detail. He returned during mid-vacation to rank the department without, however, reviewing each decision unit. The results were disappointing; his knowledge was still too general to work constructively with the third-level managers who had the in-depth understanding of the cost/benefit/consequence nature of their activities.

The department head wisely stopped and rescheduled the meeting, promising to be better prepared next time. When the meeting reconvened after two weeks, the manager not only had almost memorized each analysis, but had prepared several pad-board pages with his assumptions, operating strategy for the upcoming year, and logic by which he would rank the increments against his strategy. The result of the Marketing ranking was a logically and systematically developed budget at a level 12 percent higher than the prior year's budget.

ENGINEERING

The approach to the Engineering ranking was considerably different than that of the Marketing Department, primarily because the needs were very different. The head of Engineering had several objectives in mind for his ranking:

1. He sensed a need to encourage systems-thinking first among his own managers and secondly within the corporation as a whole. Systems-thinking in this context meant shifting the traditional functional view to one recognizing the nature of the functional contribution to the corporate or departmental whole.
2. He wanted to be assured that at any given level of expenditure his department would be balanced relative to the engineering tasks to be accomplished.
3. He wanted to spot organization weakness or critical areas in which the lack of proper emphasis today would hurt the company in the future.

To achieve these objectives it was first necessary to develop an analytical framework for the head of Engineering. It was decided that departmental decision units should be established, based on the primary systems. The head of Engineering felt there was a need to improve the knowledge about those primary systems.

Three generic activities or "systems" were identified: providing network capacity, service support, and general organizational support. These served in effect as "departmental" decision units for which the head of Engineering was the decision unit manager. Once this was accomplished, as many as 13 subelements contributing to each of the three generic activities were identified. In the case of providing network capacity they included such activities as fundamental planning, forecasting, systems design, current planning, standards, detailed engineering, budgeting, maintenance, construction, installation, and quality control.

The next step was to establish the logic by which increments of the head of Engineering decision units could be established. It was finally decided to identify four categories of increments into which all the functional increments could be slotted. They were defined as:

1. Unconditional requirements which, if not performed, would expose the Utility Company to unacceptable economic, legal, or technological risk.
2. Requirements or badly needed new activities, but not of the same relative importance as those in the first category.
3. Highly desirable activities (either existing or new) that would contribute to departmental effectiveness, both in the short and long term.
4. Activities for which the benefits were greater than the costs and should be strongly considered but which the organization may not have been able to absorb during the current budget cycle.

It was important to establish external standards against which to evaluate functional activities. This was done to avoid an intradepartmental conflict that might arise from comparing individual increments thereby diverting the ranking participants from developing a system view. Once the system that would be used to translate sectional activities into a language meaningful at the department level was selected, a series of meetings were convened with all the section heads and the departmental ranking began.

Prior to the departmental ranking, one of the most experienced third-level managers—acting for the head of Engineering—made a first attempt at slotting each functional decision unit increment into the appropriate category or categories as described above. This was done to save time as well as to show the other managers involved what the finished system would look like.

There was anything but total agreement with respect to the categorization and relative prioritization of the increments. The group then evaluated in detail each of the 135 original decision unit increments and modified their placement. Up to this point in the process the resources required (dollars and people) were not formally considered. By focusing away from monetary considerations, it was felt that more attention could be given to the planning aspect, that is, the activities required to accomplish the job at various levels of service or quality. Once all functional activities were properly categorized and ranked in the systems format, a budget summary was composed.

Upon analysis it was determined that it would cost 96.5 percent of the 1976 expenditure level to fund the combined first and second increments. The third increment could be funded for a total of 118.4 percent of 1976, while everything the department wanted to accomplish through the fourth increment would total in excess of 125 percent of 1976.

The head of Engineering recognized that the actual funding would probably fall within the third increment. But in order to ensure the company's technological position, he knew that the department should be operating within the fourth increment. He therefore decided to rank those functional increments in categories three and four against each other. To do this he felt he needed better and more quantitative performance measures. To get more detailed performance measures, he sent the analyses back to the decision unit manager for a more rigorous, quantitative cost/benefit analysis. This also reinforced the importance of the analyses. Against the cost, the managers were expected to calculate the expense dollars saved both within the department and external to it as well as the present value of capital dollars saved by more effective decision making, quality control, or planning.

FINANCIAL ACCOUNTING

This department experienced a ranking problem. Financial Accounting was basically the department responsible for the general ledger, customer records and billing functions, payroll, cost, and investment accounting departments.

The nature of the problem was organizational, but was precipitated by two inherent characteristics of the Zero-Base system: the visibility into the organization that is provided and the forum for upward communication afforded lower level managers.

Decision unit managers and lower level ranking managers revealed that the department was overstaffed with first-level managers and trainees, and that some clerical activities were being done only because they had always been done. A problem arose when the department manager, believing that the vice president—finance might question his management ability, instructed the decision unit manager through the intermediate ranking managers, to redo the analysis. He suggested that the unit managers provide less detail. This, in essence, obscured the detail originally provided. Rather than using the process to open up communication with the lower level managers and to provide an ongoing opportunity for dialogue and training, the department head viewed the process as a threat and was more concerned with the type of information he would communicate upward.

This problem was resolved only after the vice president—finance was alerted to the problem, and provided an independent analysis of the issue. The vice president—finance concluded that there was indeed a management development problem within the department and asked the department manager to present a plan to better utilize lower level managers.

Once the ranking was complete at the departmental level, preparations began for corporate level rankings. The first part in this final process was the review of each department; and then the ranking of all departments reporting to the respective vice presidents.

CORPORATE RANKINGS

There were to be two levels of ranking at the corporate level, one at the vice presidential level (operations, planning, and finance) and then the final companywide ranking. For several reasons, rankings at the top level were delayed. Like almost all utilities during 1976, the company was preparing for a new debt issue, new equity issue, and rate increase application, and was experiencing labor disruptions. It was therefore difficult for senior management to devote the required time to the process. In a way, management was relieved to be able to put off the departmental tradeoffs because this part of the process is often frustrating. Although the rankings were delayed, the preparation for them was useful in terms of adapting the Zero-Base process to the existing long-range planning system through the use of corporate key planning areas.

The idea of tying functional budgets to corporate planning via corporate key planning areas emerged in Planning Department ranking sessions. Key Planning Areas were 12 separate corporate activities usually involving more than one department. They were to be used to tie the corporation together during the comprehensive long-range planning process.

Once Key Planning Areas had been identified, interviews were conducted with the other vice presidents to determine if the concept would serve as a useful tool to enable them to make corporate budget decisions. When they became familiar with all the Key Planning Areas, the other vice presidents felt the Key Planning Area idea would be best used to supplement information as already presented functionally. A system including forms and instruction was then developed for integrating the Key Planning Area concept into the Zero-Base process. The system was similar to one that had been developed in the Engineering Department.

A series of work sheets were distributed to the department managers who were responsible for assuring that each increment analyzed during the project was slotted in the proper Key Planning Area—according to relative priority—using the same three categories already defined. Additionally, the increments were further categorized as to their nature within each Key Planning Area, that is, activities whose costs were identified as: (1) essentially load-related or in response to some external demand; (2) current support where the majority of the benefits would be achieved during the budget year; and (3) future support where the benefit of current year expenditures would be realized two to five years in the future.

Once the Key Planning Area analysis was completed, the executives had vast amounts of information available to them. Information was available in functional, department-oriented format supplemented by an executive summary prepared by the department manager. Information consisting of activities and their costs was also organized by corporate systems—as represented by Key Planning Areas—with additional systems detail provided by the Engineering Department. And, most importantly, all the information could be readily tracked to the original cost/benefit/consequence incremental analysis performed by the decision unit manager.

CONCLUSIONS

The delay in the overall ranking could have been overcome by better design of the process. By gaining greater initial top management support and foreseeing the heavy time commitments upon management time, the process could have been improved.

Heavy Equipment Division, Lindema Corporation*

In mid-1975 the controller of Heavy Equipment Division, Lindema Corporation read an article about Zero-Base Planning and Budgeting and, with other top management, made the decision to give the concept a trial.

Because of the economic crunch in the energy sector, the company was facing a decrease in volume. It was therefore essential that sizable administered costs be reduced in order to achieve acceptable profit levels and to adjust the resources to lower business levels. The concepts of the Zero-Base process seemed appropriate to these desired objectives.

A task force was assembled from within the company and immediately went to work. Their initial efforts resulted in a budgeting form which was distributed to managers within the unit along with instructions to fill out the form. However, after two or three months of trial, it was concluded that their system was not working.

Management opinion was still in favor of the concept, however, so the company elected to bring in outside help (management consultants) to work with the Controller's Department. The initial step was to collect organization charts, accounts, planning information, and financial statistics from the controller to familiarize the outside management team with the structure and financial statistics of the company. Administered or "managed" expenses totaled about $85 million. These costs and salaried employees were broken down as shown in Table 1.

TABLE 1
Administered or "managed" expenses

Organization	Number of employees	Annual costs ($000)
Engineering	822	$20,800
Marketing	46	2,300
Service	87	2,800
Materials and projects	156	2,900
Personnel	76	2,600
Controller	242	12,200
Quality control	10	220
Plant A	738	22,900
Plant B	279	9,200
Plant C	296	10,800

*The name is disguised at the request of the divisional management of this multibillion dollar company.

OBJECTIVES

Objectives for the process were identified as follows:

1. To thoroughly analyze operations involving managed costs; to make a concerted effort to identify new approaches to tasks; and to clarify the relationship between the level of services needed and the cost of providing service at different levels.
2. To provide management with a substantial data base on which to draw in making intelligent allocation decisions; to enable management to better communicate clear expectations for performance.
3. To reallocate resources among the budgets so as to reenforce the critical functions of the division without disrupting the work which had to be accomplished.
4. To design reasonable performance measurements of individual budget managers' work.
5. To train individual budget managers better in the analysis of their needs and functions.

In addition, while working on the implementation, the team was charged with isolating problem areas and issues, recognizing that some of these issues would be resolved naturally by the ranking process and that some would require special attention.

DESIGN AND IMPLEMENTATION—PLANTS C AND B

Plant C

The design phase lasted through the month of September, and the first Zero-Base Planning and Budgeting kickoff was held October 5th with the 31 managers at Plant C.

A serious implementation problem arose immediately.

It is a basic prerequisite in the Zero-Base approach that the level of business volume expected during the budget cycle be well defined. The division had a clear idea of the total apparatus capacity output that was expected during 1976; however, the individual managers had limited information regarding what this level of business meant in relationship to the individual requirements that would be placed on them personally.

A typical problem was the question of "apparatus mix." It was important to know if the apparatus to be produced in 1976 required standard designs or new designs for the product. Obviously, new designs would mean that a greater number of engineering and process designs would be needed than if standard designs could be utilized. Answering this new versus standard question became the first major challenge of the assignment.

As the implementation proceeded, individual discussions with the decision unit managers were instituted and plant managers held meetings with key engineering and manufacturing personnel to resolve these questions. Projections were run and fundamental business planning figures were reviewed. An attempt was made to forecast what service work on existing products and what types of apparatus would most likely be needed. Ultimately, this planning effort reached the highest level of manufacturing management within the division where final questions were resolved. Thus, the first contribution of Zero Base was the stimulation of better planning figures for the next budgeting cycle.

Once these business assumptions were completed the preparation of decision units could be finalized. Another major problem then surfaced. It had been the practice within the division to prorate the expenses of the staff units in headquarters to the various budgets to which the staff work was directed. Over time, however, the line managers had come to accept these prorated charges as "given." There was a concern about how to handle these prorated charges since they were unrelated to the amount of service provided.

After initial discussions it was decided to move these charges to a new entry line on the forms. Each consultant kept separate notes about the charge-backs to and from each of the decision units. Gradually questions began to emerge as to the size of the staff effort being explained through the pro rate charging. The large size of this pro rata amount indicated a possible imbalance between the staff actually in place and the total need. This staff support issue was shelved temporarily as efforts continued to complete the Zero-Base Planning and Budgeting implementation at Plant C.

Numerous issues popped up as a result of the manager's analysis and were resolved at the plant level. Some examples of these issues involved: centralization of certain functions; adequacy of the physical record-keeping systems for quality control purposes; separation of some areas of responsibility which had been previously undefined; subcontracting of certain plant functions rather than bearing the cost of full-time employees.

As the work at Plant C progressed, managers became more enthusiastic about the process. Several of them said that the special effort to develop the planning assumption would make their jobs much less uncertain. Performance measurements began to emerge which managers felt would enable them to analyze their outputs in relation to their resources, and better evaluate their own performance as managers, thereby decreasing the amount of subjectivity in the performance evaluation system.

Ranking process difficulties

The ranking process also ran into initial problems. In one instance a ranking manager, who was used to making decisions himself, gave the process a brief exposure at the first meeting, which lasted less than a half hour. He simply sorted out increments while his decision unit managers sat by quietly and observed. No discussion was encouraged by him even though the consulting team members deliberately attempted to provoke a flow of ideas on the relative rankings of some increments.

However, the decision unit managers were not easily quieted. They had worked diligently on their planning and, because they did not know what assumptions their peers had used in formulating their decision unit increments, were not satisfied that they could accept the priorities as set out by their boss. They surrounded the ranking manager outside the meeting room and requested that each be allowed to review the materials developed by the others. Ultimately this debate created enough pressure to convince the boss that he should reconvene the ranking meeting, which then ran for five hours.

After that session the decision unit managers concluded that the end result was "fair." While the "old line" manager did not emerge from the process a partisan of the new participatory style, he did gain a real measure of respect for the information generating power that peer ranking meetings could give him, and so was satisfied that the process was worthwhile.

Plant B

The Plant B implementation began in early November. The implementation difficulties paralleled those of the Plant C experience and were resolved quickly.

The ranking process, however, reflected the differing management styles of the two plants. The lower level ranking managers were younger and for the most part newer to their jobs than their counterparts at Plant C. As a result, the lower level ranking meetings were more free-flowing, characterized by a high degree of decision unit manager participation and influence. The Plant B ranking managers probably "learned" more about their operations than their counterparts at Plant C. Certainly the relative involvement of the decision unit managers prepared them to accept any resultant budget reductions.

The ranking by the plant manager, however, was completely different than that at the first plant. The Plant B manager had preconceived ideas of what should be eliminated and relied less on the information generated by the lower level managers and their suggestions than the Plant C manager.

Interestingly enough, however, the same post ranking "rebellion" took place at Plant B as had taken place at Plant C—although it occurred at the next higher level of management. Again, a reconvened meeting resulted in more participation by the staff managers.

"Funding line" ranking

Division management decided to rank this plant together with Plant C to establish the "funding line." The decision was made recognizing the proximity of year-end, and the fact that both plants had a full capacity load for the next two years, as contrasted with Plant A, at Headquarters, where the load was dramatically lower.

The ranking session for Plants B and C was abysmal. The division manager had difficulty coping with the tremendous volume of decision unit data that was available for review. Certain units were incomplete, and the lack of summary information resulted in too much general discussion as opposed to the need for focusing on critical elements for decision-making purposes. Subsequent analysis revealed several factors which influenced the situation and contributed to the marginal success of the meeting.

- The division manager had expected that far more would be developed by way of alternative ways of doing business. His expectations were not met.
- The lack of summary data in a format which could be easily assimilated clouded the results of the Zero-Base effort.
- There was a "feeling" that Zero-Base Planning and Budgeting was effective in explaining why things should be done in the way they had been rather than in new and different ways.
- The reduction potential, although present in the data base, was not accomplished by a statement regarding what organizational changes could or should be made coincident with a reduction in business volume.
- The division manager and other top managers could not easily use the data or read the forms and the discussion tended to mix the issue of the funding line with questions regarding the accuracy of the decision units.

Although the implementation team had advised the division manager that lack of an opportunity to run through a preparation step preliminary to the ranking would make the process more difficult, the level of disappointment with the meeting was not anticipated.

The situation was analyzed and the problems seemed related to three key factors:

1. The preparation steps prior to the ranking meeting had been shortchanged. The practice of using "administration decision units" separating costs for the first-level ranking manager as an increment was not being properly handled in the lower level ranking process.
2. Organizational realignments were not popping up on the ranking sheet automatically because ranking managers were giving their own personal unit high priority even when those under them were reduced drastically.
3. Management expectations for the development of alternatives were too high, possibly because of too much emphasis on this point in initial client meetings.

These problems were resolved as follows:

Inadequate preparation for ranking

The consulting team reviewed the typical consultant/decision unit manager interaction and concluded that in some cases the consultant became too involved with the logic and substance of the decision unit and missed certain omissions and mistakes. The ranking process had to be preceded by a third-party review step, and followed by an analysis of the impact of the ranked increments in summary form. A three-step ranking process was outlined which would: (a) guarantee the accuracy and completeness of data, (b) assure that ranking managers were thoroughly familiar with the substance of each decision unit, and (c) identify ways to summarize the results of the ranking for use by higher level managers.

Lack of focus on possible organizational changes

One of the characteristics inherent in the normal Zero-Base Budgeting process is the automatic realignment of functions. As the funding line is moved up and down the ranking list, some functions are either incorporated or eliminated, tending to dictate the needed organizational structure as functions fall away or are added.

But in the case of Lindema Corporation, "administrative decision units" were used to contain the salaries of the next lower management level. This practice coincided with the existing accounting system characteristics. Naturally, these administrative decision units were ranked first on any ranking of the related functional increments. The result was that while the funding level might be changed, the organizational structure tended to remain the same.

This characteristic of administration decision units to cluster toward the top of the ranking caused the division manager some concern. It seemed to indicate the absence of sufficient thought about possible organization changes which should occur at different levels of funding.

To overcome this problem the division manager instituted a span of control analysis for his general staff members and asked them to show the organizational impact at the different levels of funding recommended.

Lack of sufficient alternatives developed

Developing alternatives is always a difficult area because the implementation time used to initiate the Zero-Base Planning and Budgeting process is compressed. While alternatives are identified, often they cannot be thoroughly examined in the time allowed. To combat the lack of alternatives the consultants reemphasized this area of analysis with decision unit managers and with ranking managers.

PLANT A AND DIVISION HEADQUARTERS
SITE IMPLEMENTATION

The Plant A decision units constituted 72 percent of the total. The work began on November 19, 1975, and lasted through February 1976.

The implementation efforts encompassed elements of Manufacturing and Engineering, the controller's operations, and a number of smaller administrative departments. Most of the work proceeded in line with previous experiences in Plants B and C. The exception to this was the large Engineering Department which posed some difficulties to the team.

The Engineering Department

The Engineering organization was an 800-man department organized into five subunits: three functional, which were oriented toward development activities, engineering in support of orders received, and service work; plus two support groups, laboratories and computer services, and an administrative group which included drafting support. The source of many of the problems which were encountered arose not only from the structure of the traditional budgeting process but also from the particular culture of the organization.

The Engineering Department was a relatively closed environment with a substantial percentage of the staff, both management and professional, made up of veterans of 20-35 years' service in the department. The "stability" of the Engineering Department—relative to other parts of the division, as well as divisional management itself—led to a situation in which that department had developed, over a period of time, into the "conscience" of the company. The result was that the Engineering Department appeared to be somewhat overstaffed relative to the company's current engineering requirements.

Many of the implementation problems paralleled those at the other plants. One significant problem in engineering was a common attitude that Zero-Base Planning and Budgeting was an accounting exercise and that the results, while potentially interesting, would not be implemented within the department. It became apparent by the second meeting with decision unit managers that the visible support of both the departmental manager and divisional general manager was lacking—at least as perceived by decision unit managers. In other words, the process had not been "legitimatized" in the eyes of the decision unit manager. The consulting team explained their concerns to the engineering manager during a morning progress meeting and by mid-afternoon, decision unit managers were working with a different perspective.

The traditional exclusion of the first-level engineering managers (decision unit managers) from the planning process caused them significant problems with many of the analytical aspects of the process. Specifically, most of the decision unit managers had difficulty placing priorities; i.e., making trade-offs among the various activities that they were responsible for, making quantity/quality decisions relative to levels of service, and developing sound and meaningful performance measures.

At this point it became clear that the Zero-Base process could contribute a great deal in improving the decision unit manager's business orientation. The lack of business orientation on the part of the decision unit managers which made quality/quantity trade-offs virtually impossible was overcome by introducing the notion of increasing turnabout times, backlogs and forcing the prioritization of customer requests according to economic impact. For example, at a reduced level of funding, decision units in service engineering would service 100 percent of contractual obligations, but increase turnaround time on requests from nonpaying customers and licensees. Additionally, marketing would be required to identify customers with the greatest potential to ensure prompt servicing of them while reducing the priority for customers with sales potential below a certain dollar amount. Similarly the decision unit's support of manufacturing would be reduced by increasing the backlog of requests for engineering support and the support of marketing negotiations would be reduced from an on-demand basis to one which would require marketing to schedule and prioritize negotiation support requests.

In other areas which were staffed to handle peak loads and crises, decision unit managers used the Zero-Base Planning and Budgeting process to communicate to management that at a reduced level of funding, problem-solving task forces would have to be provided from various parts of the organization to respond to high priority crises, and that management would be required to help coordinate the formation of these task forces as needed. The decision unit managers were then faced with the usual decisions regarding which activity to improve as people and dollar resources were added, decisions which, at this point, came relatively easily.

The problem of developing appropriate work load and performance measures was only partially remedied and was ultimately defined as an improvement area to be worked on after the process was implemented. The Zero-Base process confirmed management's feelings that the lower level engineering managers were oriented toward working on problems and trying to find optimal solutions—not toward defining adequate cost-effective solutions at given resource levels.

In summary, the majority of the decision unit managers not only submitted well-thought-out decision unit analyses, but also seemed to gain insight into planning and the requirement of making judgmental business decisions.

FINAL RANKING

After the engineering decision units were brought to a satisfactory level of completion, and the other departments' units were completed, a schedule of meetings was drawn up. The agenda for these meetings included a description by the ranking manager of the work that had been accomplished and his recommendation of a funding level appropriate to the business volume expected. The consultants were asked to comment on their findings related to a review of budget requests relative to last year's actual usage; an appraisal of how well decision units had been prepared; an analysis of how funds would shift between departments at three different levels of funding; and, finally, a list of issues and concerns which the consultants felt should be discussed.

These preranking meetings also gave the managers a chance to gain insight into the operations of each department and its decision units prior to the group ranking. Many important issues were discussed at these meetings.

Some ranking managers came to the meetings with differently formulated information and were requested to complete a presentation to their peers in the joint meeting which was planned.

The first joint meeting was held in the division conference room and was an all-day affair. Each ranking staff manager made a formal presentation of his budget recommendations, and the ideas which had been developed to save money. By the end of the meeting the division manager had a very good perspective on the level and the amount of thinking which had been devoted and was not fully satisfied. He established an offsite location for a final meeting and challenged his staff managers to come to the meeting prepared with numerous good ideas for cost reductions, business improvements, and organizational consolidations. They would have a week to prepare.

THE LAST MEETING

The final ranking meeting began at 8 a.m. in a nearby hotel. A peer vote by secret ballot established the relative order of departments who had the most "fat" in their organization (the engineers "won" with 8.5 on a scale of 1 to 10). Throughout the day the walls of the conference room were gradually papered over with drawing pad paper covered in felt tip markings. By evening, eight ideas were isolated, each of which constituted a major change either in resource usage or organizational alignment. Most important, however, was the fact that there was some contribution from every manager in every one of these major activity areas, which included computer usage, combinations of resources, marketing strategy, personnel reallocations, and shifting and realignment of several functions between staff managers.

A budget was drawn up from the individual ranking of each staff manager. The sum of the budgets was 10 percent below the previously established company target for cost reduction even before the eight major cost saving ideas could be implemented. In addition, the budgets for each manager differed significantly from the individual targets established for each area. The managers learned enough from the Zero-Base process to change their preconceived ideas about both the magnitude of the overall reduction and the areas where the reductions would be achieved.

The voluminous flow of ideas during the day was gradually reduced to a few major idea groupings. Assignments were made to individual managers to formulate action plans in each of these areas. Budgets were roughly established which ranged from budget increases for some areas to a plan to reduce engineering costs by 20 percent over the coming budgeting cycle.

The reduction for the entire division was ultimately over 25 percent. This major reduction was possible partially because business volume was significantly lower in 1976.

Ottawa Area

Ottawa Area, a division of the Canadian Broadcasting Corporation, is responsible for preparing and presenting local radio and television programs in both English and French. Radio operations began during the 1930s and television operations began in the mid-1950s.

Ottawa Area maintains four radio stations: AM-English; AM-French; FM-English; and FM-French. There are two television stations in operation, one for each language. While a variety of network and local programming is presented to the public, emphasis in local programming is placed on news and current affairs.

Prior to 1968, the Head Office at the Canadian Broadcasting Corporation had centralized control over Ottawa Area operations. A decision was made in 1968 to appoint a director who would be responsible for the division's operations.

Although operations have remained decentralized since 1968, the Ottawa Area budget continues to be financed largely by the Head Office. (The Head Office derives most of its funds from the Canadian government.) In 1975, Ottawa Area's cost of operations totaled $12.7 million, of which $9.8 million was funded by the Head Office. The remaining $2.9 million was derived from commercial sales.

At the time of the 1968 decentralization a major reorganization of Ottawa Area took place. Since that time, however, it had been a fairly static organization. Planning and budget control were maintained by the director and chief accountant, with limited consultation down the line. Department heads normally had their budgets approved on the basis of last year's budget plus a percentage increment. There had been little discussion about alternate uses of public funds. Ottawa Area operated on the assumption that last year's activities would be continued while new activities would be added by the director as funds became available.

The new director suspected that Ottawa Area had been funding a number of nonessential activities while ignoring urgent new opportunities. A significant reallocation of funds was probably needed, but this was unlikely under the traditional budgeting system. Because of the nature of this budgeting system, department heads tended to ask for larger funding than was really required in order to assure that they would still be left with an adequate operating budget following the inevitable cutbacks.

OBJECTIVES

Gordon Bruce had been director of Ottawa Area for less than a year when he decided to implement Zero-Base Budgeting in 1975. He had several objectives in mind.

1. To transfer funds from low-priority to high-priority areas.

2. To develop a planning process within Ottawa Area to include an examination of new alternative ways of operating.

3. To educate management in the budgetary process through a greater analytical orientation.

4. To learn in detail about the functions of the various departments and to highlight problem areas.

5. To develop better communication among management through the identification of Ottawa Area goals.

6. To develop an integrated planning process that would be self-perpetuating.

Gordon Bruce realized that most of his managers had worked at Ottawa Area for several years. However, he felt that some of them did not actually "manage." They were not looking for better ways to operate; they had not established standards against which performance could be measured; and they tended to accept past procedures instead of analyzing them.

Bruce believed Zero-Base Planning and Budgeting would allow him to review his departments' operations thoroughly in a relatively short time. He felt that this system would enable him to make needed changes on a rational basis, and would readily complement the management by objectives and financial analysis systems already in place.

Prior to the introduction of Zero Base at Ottawa Area, the chief accountant and production manager had been trying to relate the program schedule for the coming year to the resources (cameras, cameramen, studios, stagehands, and so on) available to meet the schedule. From the schedule and from discussions with various producers, the needed resources were to be determined. The available resources would then be compared with the demand, with the end result being a schedule for the coming year. Attached to each resource would be a costing rate, which was reflected on the user department's budget.

The procedure used to prepare the resource schedule is known as a capacity cost system. The director felt that a capacity cost system for programming aspects combined with a Zero-Base Planning and Budgeting system for overhead aspects would provide Ottawa Area with an effective management planning system.

DESIGN AND IMPLEMENTATION

Zero-Base Planning and Budgeting was applied only to the pure overhead areas initially. These areas included: engineering; finance; sales; personnel; public relations;

and administrative services. It was believed that the programming departments would not be conducive to the process.

The decision unit managers' reaction to Zero Base was cautiously enthusiastic. They agreed that a process like this was ideal for communicating their ideas to the director. They knew he was committed to the process and that they consequently had a "pipeline to the top."

UNION PROBLEMS

A major problem during the implementation was the large role that unions play throughout the Canadian Broadcasting Corporation. Both hourly workers and clerical staff are union members. Ottawa Area had negotiated a contract with the union that greatly inhibited management's ability to discharge employees. Employee misconduct, which was very difficult to substantiate, was one of the few reasons for staff dismissal. Management found grievance meetings time consuming and often unsuccessful. But the union problem was not insurmountable.

Initially, when decision unit managers at Ottawa Area were asked to propose alternative operating plans and to discuss the feasibility of the plans, they frequently cited "union constraints" as an inhibiting factor. Rather than accepting this excuse, the Zero-Base Planning and Budgeting process was used to question whether or not the alternatives were satisfactory under nonunion conditions. It turned out that the union excuse was overplayed. As one candid and objective manager commented: "It is very easy to blame the union for all our troubles, but that is neither practical nor realistic. We need new ideas—the 'union problem' can be reckoned with."

When alternatives were considered viable and union constraints prevented them from being used, they were documented and communicated to the director. Consequently, when the next union contract is negotiated, management will have some additional objectives in mind when bargaining begins.

EXTENSION OF THE PROCESS

After Zero-Base analyses for the six overhead areas were completed, Ottawa Area had intended to conclude implementation of the process. A detailed review of the organization chart, however, revealed that several activities within the technical and programming areas were not subject to a capacity cost system. These included all administrative functions within the radio and television departments and the publicity function. Subsequently, Zero-Base Planning and Budgeting was applied effectively to each of these areas.

Positions such as cameramen and stagehands were not analyzed because these were strictly related to programming plans. There was no way, for example, to evaluate the effect of reducing the number of technicians from 150 to 125 without referring to actual programming needs. And, as Ottawa Area is primarily a current events and news vehicle, complete programming requirements for the year cannot be anticipated.

It was felt that some managers would regard Zero-Base Planning and Budgeting as a mere exercise, soon to be forgotten. Consequently, at an early stage of implementation, Gordon Bruce informed the decision unit managers that they should regard the process as a management planning tool. He indicated that he would personally review each analysis critically and would build the upcoming year's plan on the basis of the analyses.

In several departments the number of decision units greatly exceeded initial expectations. For example, the head of the Administrative Services Department had responsibility for eight decision units: (1) office services communications, (2) records management, (3) transportation, (4) mail, (5) duplicating, (6) purchasing, (7) stores, and (8) building services. However, Bruce's guideline of preparing "grass-root" analyses warranted identification of as many decision units as practical. Since the staff level associated with each of these activities was large enough to warrant separate decision units, the additional analytical time was justified. Throughout the Ottawa Area, Zero-Base analyses took place at the lowest managerial levels possible and required the involvement of employees at every level in the managerial group.

Ranking

After all decision unit analyses had been completed, the decision unit managers met with Bruce individually. Each increment was reviewed critically with the director questioning the logic of the increment content and sequence. He was particularly concerned with one decision unit manager who had placed a few relatively low-priority activities in the minimum increment in an attempt to sneak through some "pet" projects. This decision unit manager had, no doubt, assumed that all minimum increments would be funded automatically. At the same time he had deliberately left out of the minimum increment certain essential basic activities which he also assumed would then have to be funded by one means or another. The review by Bruce tended to minimize this type of "games-playing."

After Bruce was satisfied with each analysis he told the decision unit manager which of his increments would definitely be funded in 1976. When this was performed for all decision units, he assembled all of his managers as a group to rank those increments that were discretionary. He knew that his approved 1976 funding level for overhead activities was $4,300,000. Prior to the group ranking meeting, he had already consented to fund increments valued at $3,600,000. Hence the first $700,000 worth of increments to be ranked would be funded. The ranking of the discretionary increments was participative, with the group generally agreeing on the relative priorities of the increments.

After ranking had been determined, it was noted that presently funded items totaling $102,000 were ranked below the funding line. Bruce stated that these items would be financed on a temporary basis, but emphasized that regulation of these "problems" would be necessary if the budget target was to be met. The decision unit managers responsible for these items were then asked to determine their plans of action.

CONCLUSION AND SUMMARY

In summarizing the benefits that Ottawa Area derived from the Zero Base, Gordon Bruce recently said: "Our managers are more budget conscious now, and they possess a greater awareness of their operations. In general, Ottawa Area has accomplished a better allocation of funds."

Although the process was perceived favorably in most cases, a few participants complained about the seemingly heavy time commitment that was required of them. In addition, there were some comments that alternatives should have received greater emphasis to encourage creativity on the part of the managers.

The tangible benefits associated with the Zero-Base Planning and Budgeting effort at Ottawa Area are as follow:

1. Improved scheduling of transportation service allowed for a reduction in vehicles and staff. Resultant cost savings were $20,000 per year.
2. Funding for a planned major reorganization and expansion of the training department was identified.
3. Support staff were transferred from low-priority to high-priority activities.
4. Three positions were eliminated.

Equally tangible, but less quantifiable, was the effect of the ranking process, which required all senior managers to give serious thought to the administrative needs of Ottawa Area and to cooperate as objectively as possible in the establishment of priorities.

At the conclusion of Ottawa Area's first Zero-Base Planning and Budgeting implementation, Gordon Bruce sent a memorandum to all of the decision unit managers. The final paragraph read: "I feel that we now have a rational framework for the administrative aspect of our activities, and I am convinced that the result of this (Zero-Base implementation) will be much greater efficiency in the utilization of the funds allotted to us."

In commenting on the benefits of the process as he perceived them, the chief accountant said: "While the Zero-Base Planning and Budgeting process has some immediate values, the main thrust of its benefit to us will be in future years. The planning benefits should be ongoing. This is not a one-time exercise."

POSTSCRIPT

In the spring of 1976, Ottawa Area entered its second Zero-Base Planning and Budgeting cycle. In the second year, the analytical effort required by decision unit managers was reduced by 40 percent and the process became easier to implement.

One of the factors leading to a smoother process in 1976 was the redesign of the system based on the 1975 experience. The new design streamlined paper work and increased the emphasis on cost/benefit trade-offs. One manager summarized the second year's effort: "This year's effort (1976) institutionalized the effort we went through last year (1975). Next year (1977) should be a breeze."

case five

Allied Van Lines

Allied Van Lines, an international moving and storage company, is the 11th largest motor carrier in the United States. Its International and Special Products operations are growing rapidly.

Until 1969, Allied Van Lines was structured as a nonprofit organization. In May 1969, the business charter was changed to create a standard business organization. Two classes of stock were issued: Class A, the voting stock, can be traded only by the agents to whom it was issued; and Class B, a nonvoting stock, is traded publicly in the over-the-counter market.

Prior to the change in charter in 1969, Allied functioned largely as a service organization for agents. It maintained a dispatch center and handled agent bookings. This was done on a service-center basis by which agents paid for the cost of service rendered; i.e., Allied made no profit on services.

It was anticipated that the installation of a profit motive would lead to a more effective organization—one with the ability to earn profits and grow. However, despite the radical change in charter, the performance from 1969 to 1975 was undistinguished. Sales grew rapidly, but profits did not because management was unable to control overhead costs, which grew faster than sales. Table 1 provides a historical perspective on Allied's sales and profit growth during the period from 1967 to 1975.

TABLE 1
Financial results for Allied Van Lines Corporation

Year	Net sales ($ millions)	Service and administrative expense ($ millions)	Service and administrative expense (percent of sales)	Earnings per share ($)
1967	$134.9	$ 7.8	5.78%	— *
1968	147.9	9.2	6.22	— *
1969	168.7	10.4	6.16	— *
1970	170.2	10.9	6.40	$0.46
1971	172.9	11.3	6.54	1.19
1972	187.3	12.1	6.46	1.28
1973	199.6	13.2	6.61	0.60
1974	236.4	15.9	6.73	0.51
1975	224.0	17.5	7.81	0.42

*Funds returned to agents pursuant to Allied's "not for profit" charter.
Source: Allied Van Lines Annual Reports.

OBJECTIVES

In May 1975, the board of directors elected a new president, Jack Schang, formerly executive vice president at North American Van Lines. Soon after taking over as president, Schang decided to implement Zero-Base Planning and Budgeting at Allied. At the time of his decision, Schang had three major concerns. First, as a newcomer, he was not familiar with all aspects of the Allied operation. An in-depth look at the organization would allow an overall examination and provide a close examination of the managers' analytical skills.

Schang was also concerned about the overhead dollars being spent. He expected a step function as sales increased; i.e., overhead dollars should have remained constant at a level and then increased. However, as shown in the third column of Table 1, those costs increased as a percent of sales over time. In 1975, when sales dropped, overhead continued to increase. Schang wanted to understand the nature of those costs in order to explain this phenomenon.

The new executive's third problem was that the base business had not been examined in recent years. After several months on the job, he discovered that there were many duplicative functions being performed and that potentially high payoff projects and opportunities were not being identified and funded.

Zero-Base Planning and Budgeting was to be implemented throughout the company with the project to begin in early August and to be completed in mid-October in time for the annual budget presentation.

DESIGN AND IMPLEMENTATION

A project team was established that included four outside consultants and one member of Allied's profit planning staff. The design of the appropriate Zero-Base Planning and Budgeting system was undertaken in July and completed in early August. As part of the design process, 76 decision units were identified. They were divided among the various functional areas as shown in Table 2.

Following the identification of the decision units and their respective managers, Robert Seeler, the controller, published a memorandum identifying the major planning

TABLE 2
Allied Van Lines decision units

Functional area	Number of decision units
Finance	24
Administration	13
Legal	10
International	8
Management Science and Information Services	8
Omaha Operations	6
Marketing	4
Special Products	2
Executive	1
Total	76

assumptions for fiscal 1976. Domestic volume of household shipments was expected to increase by 10 percent. International volume was expected to be up by 13.5 percent and the Special Products Department (which was just beginning operations) was expected to achieve $4.6 million in revenues in 1976. The Special Products Division was established to move complex electronic equipment and machinery.

The implementation process was started August 8 with a meeting of all decision unit managers and the project team. Individual meetings with decision unit managers began that afternoon. The project was structured so that the individual managers were scheduled to meet with the project team a minimum of five times. The team was also "on call" to decision unit managers if more meetings were deemed necessary.

Some major problems within the company surfaced as the project progressed.

1. Duplicative and outmoded training functions were discovered.
2. Duplicative marketing function with no clear policy was uncovered.
3. Both central and decentralized approaches to purchasing were found.
4. The control and performance measurement systems were found to be outmoded and unused.

The project team attempted to bring the most relevant issues to management's attention as "issues needing resolution" before completion of the project. The resolution of other minor problems was postponed until after the new plan was in effect.

The general budgeting skills of the managers were at a rather low level primarily because budgeting had been a "top-down" affair prior to Zero-Base Planning and Budgeting. Now managers were being asked to develop their own budgets. Most of them enthusiastically accepted the challenge and several good ideas emerged, for example:

- Allied's Insurance group used the process to propose an expanded insurance marketing program to top management.
- The manager of Personnel used Zero Base to analyze Allied's employee insurance coverage.
- The implications of offering national and government account financing to agents were examined in the Accounting Department.
- All managers involved in day-to-day contact with agents—four separate groups of field personnel—reevaluated their objectives and considered alternative ways of providing service to the agents with fewer field personnel.

RANKING

After completion of the analysis and preparation of the decision unit forms in draft, the results were reviewed with the first-level ranking managers to ensure that decision unit managers were "on track." The next step was to develop expense budgets by increment. After this step was completed, the manager of Profit Planning reviewed the budgets to ensure the accuracy of salaries and cost elements.

The ranking process, which began in mid-September, was divided into three levels: first level, managers; second level, vice presidents; third level, chief executive. The managerial ranking served two purposes: it provided the managers with an opportunity for a last look at the decision unit analysis before presentation to top management and, most importantly, it provided them with an opportunity to prioritize all of the activities under their control and to propose a ranked set to top management. Six rankings occurred at this level.

The next step was the second-level ranking in which the vice presidents reviewed all documents and developed a set of prioritized increments. This step did not go smoothly. Some of the ranking vice presidents were concerned that the logic and selection of minimum increments was not clear. A series of individual meetings were held in which the vice presidents personally reviewed all forms with the decision unit manager and his manager. In many cases, the purpose of the meeting was simply a review. In several cases, however, a completely revised decision unit analysis was prepared.

The final ranking meetings were held the following week. Each meeting was chaired by Jack Schang and attended by the appropriate vice president, the controller, the consultant assisting the decision unit manager, and the decision unit manager. By having the decision unit manager discuss his objectives, alternatives, methods of operations, and levels of service and performance measurements, a complete and detailed picture of the entire operation was presented. By studying the analysis and listening to the manager make his presentation, Jack Schang was able to evaluate his management personnel. Lastly, Schang was able to see the budget development at the "grass-roots" level.

RESULTS

The Zero-Base approach resulted in a total budget approximately 10 percent higher than the previous year's budget. The increase was due to the funding of those discretionary projects which would enable Allied to meet its profit goals. One of the projects was the staffing of the Special Products Division with both personnel and equipment. Also, Allied's Air Freight (CAB) operation was identified as an area with high profit potential. Internally, the Management Science group and Information Services were seen to have high payoff opportunities.

Table 3 compares the 1975 forecast figures and actual figures with the 1976 Zero-Base Budgeting plan for the corporation as a whole. Table 4 shows the increased funding for 1976 areas.

The ranking of activities and their costs provided the basis for Allied's 1976 Plan. Schang used the ranking table in such a way as to provide flexibility and to permit effective contingency planning. He then drew a "tight" budget line which established what he called "his profit assurance program." This was emphasized because of the nature of the moving and storage business which is both seasonal (more household

TABLE 3
Allied Van Line's 1975 operating budget plan versus actual; 1976 Zero-Base Budgeting (ZBB) Plan ($ millions)

	1975 forecast	1975 actual	1976 ZBB plan	Increase
AVL (including claims)	$16.74	$16.02	$18.40	$1.66
AVLIC (international)	1.44	1.57	1.60	0.16
AVLIA (insurance)	0.14	0.15	0.23	0.09
Totals	$18.32	$17.74	$20.23	$1.91

TABLE 4
Discretionary projects identified and funded ($ thousands)

	1975 actual	1976 ZBB plan	Increase
CAB (air freight)	0	$ 329	$329
Special Products	$ 57	285	228
Management Science	40	292	252
Information Services	1,569	1,910	341

moves occur in the spring and summer), and cyclical (because of close ties to the economy).

This contingency planning in October was of paramount importance. The value of the ranking table was that the discretionary, but extremely important, new projects and new opportunities could be funded in a timely fashion as the year unfolded, thus enabling the corporation to fund these activities consistent with profit goals.

Allied's top management realized other benefits: the business had been closely examined; managers had been identified and trained; and funds had been reallocated to potentially high profit areas. In commenting upon the implementation of Zero-Base Planning and Budgeting at Allied, Jack Schang said, "It gives top management a rapid means of grasping the key issues of the business and quickly permits resources to be squared with reality."

GenRad, Inc.*

It's been one hell of a lot of work, but I finally know what I'm supposed to be doing!

This comment, according to Steven Stadler, treasurer and chief financial officer, was the typical reaction from managers throughout the company to the ongoing efforts to institute a comprehensive system of planning and budgeting in GenRad, Inc. He and William Thurston, GenRad's president and chief executive officer, were delighted with the recent accomplishments resulting from these efforts. At the same time, these men recognized that much remained to be done to complete the design and implementation of this vital management system.

GenRad, Inc. was a privately owned corporation engaged in the design, manufacture, and sale of electronic instrumentation. Its major product categories included: instruments and systems for testing electronic circuits and components; equipment for measuring and analyzing noise and vibration; audiometric devices for dealing with speech and hearing problems; and computer-controlled systems for testing high frequency integrated circuitry.

To deal with this range of products, the company was organized with four product divisions. Exhibit 1 shows these units in a partial organization chart of the corporation. The marketing and operations departments shown in the organization chart handled sales and manufacturing for the Electronic Instrument Division (EID), the Test Systems Division (TSD), and a major part of the volume of the Enviromedics Division (EMD). Time/Data, located on the West Coast, was largely self-contained, except that its business in Europe was handled by the corporate Marketing/International Department. In 1975, GenRad employed about 1,500 men and women. The company enjoyed good employee relations. Relationships within professional ranks—management and technical—were congenial, and these people customarily addressed each other on a first-name basis.

Corporate offices and major manufacturing facilities were located in Massachusetts. Other manufacturing plants were located in California and Paris, France. Marketing offices were located in eight states, five European countries, and Canada. For 1975,

GenRad reported sales of $53.5 million and profits of $2.35 million. Exhibit 2 gives a summary of recent financial results.

EVENTS LEADING TO MANAGEMENT CHANGES

Founded in 1915 under the name General Radio Company,[1] the firm grew to be the largest and most respected manufacturer of electrical measurement and test apparatus in the United States by the late 1930s.[2] The years during and following World War II, however, were to see General Radio's competitors outstrip its growth in sales volume. By 1953, Hewlett-Packard had caught up with General Radio to share the honor for the industry's largest sales volume. By 1973, Hewlett-Packard's sales level was some 20 times greater.

During this period of time, General Radio also came to experience a steady decline in its earnings. Lower profits, culminating with a loss in 1972 (see Exhibit 2), triggered a series of moves in the company which were to change the whole management structure.

The first such change was the creation of business teams to superimpose a marketplace viewpoint on the traditional technological orientation of the company. Two years later, in December 1972, William Thurston was promoted from head of marketing and business areas to president and chief operating officer. By 1974, Mr. Thurston was well underway to changing General Radio's organization and method of operation from "... what was once suitable for a much smaller, slowly growing company, operating in a low-competition environment, to what is needed for a larger, faster growing enterprise in a highly competitive environment subject to rapid technological and market changes."

A SYSTEM OF MANAGEMENT

Faced with the need to improve the company's performance, Mr. Thurston saw the need to develop "a comprehensive and integrated, effective system of management throughout the company as soon as this could be accomplished." This system of management was to encompass corporate objectives, planning and control, organizational structure, staffing and staff development, incentive systems, and other relevant concerns.

Mr. Thurston first focused attention on developing a set of corporate objectives and strategies. By 1975, management was called upon to develop supporting objectives

[1] The firm changed its name to GenRad, Inc. on January 1, 1976.
[2] In 1942, General Radio had 287 employees, 75,000 square-feet floor space, and sales of $3.8 million.

and programs as a means of implementing the corporate guidelines. Mr. Thurston drew the preceding schematic to show the relationship of these and subsequent activities. Each of these components for planning and control will be described in turn.

CORPORATE OBJECTIVES AND STRATEGIES

A statement of corporate objectives and strategies was seen as the starting point for planning and control and for the overall comprehensive management system. In July 1975, Mr. Thurston issued the GR Annual Operations Plan describing 39 such guidelines. These were grouped under the general headings: (1) corporate mission; (2) finance and operations; (3) growth; (4) management; and (5) people. A summary list of the corporate strategies and objectives, as given in the report, is contained in Exhibit 3. Excerpts from this 41 page document follow below to illustrate the nature of these guidelines.

The operations plan began with a definition of the *Corporate Mission:*

> GR's mission is to be a free-standing, healthy business enterprise with the central purpose of enabling its people to achieve substantial economic gains and other important accomplishments for the enterprise and its owners, and for themselves as individuals, within a broad essential market offering of electronic instrumentation and associated services. Efforts will be mainly focused on more narrowly defined areas of business, selected and handled in order to build strong market positions with substantial economic diversity and the major functions performed will continue to be the surveillance of technology and customer needs, the definition of new products and services, their development, manufacture, sale and after-sale services, all managed so as to accomplish the objectives of the enterprise.

The text went on to explain in some detail the implications of this statement and to give reasons in support of this choice of mission. For example, it pointed out:

> ... the industry itself is generally predicted to be one of the fastest growing industries during the next few decades at least. There is, therefore, no pressure arising from the general need to grow that would justify the added risk of any diversion of our activity into areas beyond our broad and diversified, traditional, essential market offering. ...

In view of the financial results in recent years, special attention was given to ways of increasing profitability rapidly (GR 5.7, Exhibit 3). One means for so doing was to improve the company's inventory control system (GR 5.8, Exhibit 3).[3] On this issue, the operations plan stated:

> The Company's production inventory and control systems, procedures, practices, and attitudes, developed over many years, have led to extremely inefficient utilization of inventory.

[3]The case will illustrate the flow of information connecting the initial corporate objectives to resulting specific action programs by tracing the major references to inventory control. The data for this one issue have been severely reduced for this purpose. Comparable streams of information were prepared in the company for approximately 80 programs.

This situation has been further compounded by the existence of many low-volume products, by under-standardization of materials and components, by lack of coordination between marketing forecasts, assembly orders and production plans, and by the lack of effective controls over finished inventory diverted for demonstrators, consignment, etc.

*   *   *   *   *

In support of the strategy of greatly reducing inventory goals should be set relative to progress on the GRAPICS[4] project, and additional goals and programs should be developed in connection with:

1. Control of the forecasting process and the consistency of forecasts, "build" orders, and turn-in/shipping plans.
2. Safety-stock policies and practices.
3. Production-cycle shortening.
4. Discontinuance policies.
5. Control of Demonstrator and consignment inventories and other diversions of finished products, including the process of servicing and return/disposal.
6. Component standardization.
7. All other factors affecting inventory levels.

PRELIMINARY GOALS (MANAGEMENT BY OBJECTIVES)

The second step in the planning and control process was to translate corporate objectives and strategies into supporting operating and functional goals. In concept, each manager was to lay out the goals that he or she would have to accomplish in support of his or her superior's goals. At each lower level of management, goals generally became more specific and operational in nature. Separate goals were to be developed for ongoing operations, for solving problems, and for innovative activities.

To launch this process of setting subsidiary goals, Mr. Thurston issued on August 26, 1975 a memorandum which delegated responsibility for each of the 39 numbered Corporate Objectives and Strategies (Exhibit 3) to the 11 top corporate managers. Exhibit 4 shows one page of the accompanying work sheets used for this purpose. The memorandum text included comments about these assignments. For inventory control, the following instructions were given in the memorandum:

GR 5.8—Greatly Reduce Inventory. This Strajective is of enormous importance to the reduction of debt. Its accomplishment is delegated as follows:

1. To SJS, for documenting and implementing inventory write-off policies, and for directing, coordinating, and expediting the regular availability of inventory-responsibility reports that are satisfactory for goal-setting and performance-measurement and reward purposes,
2. To MLB, for raw materials, parts, and in-process inventories, except for G-S-brand and T/D products,

---

[4] GRAPICS (GR Automated Production and Inventory Control System) was the name given to an elaborate software package which was being designed to handle all manufacturing data, including purchasing, labor, materials, inventory, plant capacity, and so on.

3. To JFJ, for those finished and replacement-parts inventories which are under the control of GRID, the District Offices, Exhibits, and Service (re-cycling pool),
4. To JCP, DHL, EPM and SDB, for all raw, in-process, finished and marketing inventories over which they have control, or which they substantially affect through their forecasting or other decisions.

Note that a prerequisite to a satisfactory inventory-responsibility system is the very careful and explicit identification and specification of all situations in which two or more managers affect certain inventory levels through decisions or actions taken in their respective areas of responsibility, together with possibly innovative techniques for separating the effects on inventory of individual decisions to as great an extent as feasible.

Each senior level manager in turn prepared a statement of goals to correspond with the issues delegated by Thurston. As can be seen in Exhibit 4 and in the instructions quoted above, 7 of the 11 senior managers had been assigned related responsibilities for inventory control. Exhibit 5 contains excerpts from the statement of goals prepared by one of these men, the chief financial officer (SJS above).[5] In like manner, Exhibit 6 contains the goals most relevant to inventory control as set forth by Martin Blake (MLB above), vice president for Operations.

As Thurston had done, each of these senior level managers then delegated responsibility for each goal to his subordinates so that these men and women could in turn develop goals.

Within Operations, the Production and Inventory Control Department was to carry a major responsibility for achieving the desired reduction in inventory. As part of goal-setting, the following definition of the department's mission was formally stated:

Production & Inventory Control is responsible for optimized control and use of inventory in raw, parts and work-in-process inventories to meet the corporate unit objectives for cost, quality and schedule adherence improvement. Is further responsible for the successful implementation of GRAPICS during 1976.

Mr. C. J. Landry, manager of PIC, next prepared statements interpreting and elaborating the responsibilities assigned him by Mr. Blake.

PROGRAMS: ZERO-BASE FUNDING

When objectives and goals had been set for the coming year, management turned to the task of identifying and evaluating programs of action to achieve these aims. All manufacturing and selling operations, new product introductions and overhead activities were covered in this effort.

The decision unit. The programming and Zero-Base funding (ZBF)[6] at GenRad involved four basic steps. The first was to define specific cost activities so that each

---

[5] The problem solving and innovative goals listed on page 2 of the exhibit bore direct relation to inventory control.
[6] Zero-Base funding was based on the Zero-Base Budgeting concept.

could be evaluated and ranked against all other cost activities competing for resources. Two examples of such cost activities would be computer operations for administrative information systems and production inspection activities. Each such cost activity was called a "decision unit."

In a majority of cases, decision units corresponded to normal cost centers at GenRad. In some instances, decision units included several cost centers, and in others, a single cost center included more than one decision unit. The general guideline followed in defining a decision unit was that it be large enough to provide a flexibility of action, and small enough to be manageable. Eventually, about 80 decision units were identified for the company as a whole.

The second step was for each manager directly responsible for a decision unit to analyze it on a cost-benefit basis. This analysis was to address the following three questions:

1. Is the service (or program) necessary?
2. Is there a better way to accomplish this operation?
3. What different levels of service and cost are possible?

The results of this analysis were then to be reported on a series of special forms, collectively referred to as a decision package. The decision package for overhead items was to contain the following specific information.

Description of the current method of operation and its benefits.

Identification of alternative ways of achieving the required service and the advantages and disadvantages of each.

Indication of the preferred alternative.

Definition of the minimum level of activity and the related output and cost (for 1975, the minimum level was to be less than 85 percent of the current level for an ongoing activity. This measure related to dollars, or if more appropriate for a given activity, to number of positions);

Definition of several other levels of operation including the current level with related incremental outputs of service and cost.

Correlation of the increments of service to the output goals developed in MBO.

Exhibit 7 contains an abridged version of the decision package for the inventory planning and control decision unit.

Ranking the decision package increments. For Zero-Base funding, once the decision packages had been prepared, all alternative activities (the minimum and incremental levels for each package) had to be compared and ranked (step 3). In practice, each manager who received more than one decision package from subordinates had to rank all the component alternatives or increments from first to last. As these rankings moved to higher levels of management, they were combined into new composite rankings. For example, H. Putnam developed and ranked eight decision increments for Inventory Planning and Control. C. J. Landry had to rank some 22 increments for Production and Inventory Control, including the 8 from Putnam. In like manner, M. L. Blake had 152 increments to rank for the Operations Department, and W. R. Thurston had primary responsibility for ranking about 350 increments.[7] Exhibits 8, 9, and 10 show excerpts from the ranking at each successive level of management. Items relating to the inventory control issue have been noted in the exhibits.

Once the alternatives had been ranked, the incremental costs for each were totaled cumulatively in accordance with the ranked order. It was then a simple step (in theory) to draw the cut-off line at the point where available money was exhausted (step 4). All activities above the line were implemented; all below the line were rejected. If additional funds became available, a corresponding number of additional activities could be activated.

To ease the burden of ranking a large number of alternatives, many of which were quite disparate in nature, a procedure of dealing with them as groups was followed. Close attention to ranking was reserved for the group of increments falling near the possible cut-off point. Alternatives which were obligatory or highly desirable and alternatives which fell well below the cut-off point were not carefully ranked among themselves.

BUDGETING

At the conclusion of Zero-Base funding, the cost data were recast to build up the budgets for the year. Under ZBF, costs were collected for projects and programs, some of which cut across organizational lines. The budget organized costs for organizational units.

ASSESSMENTS AND ASPIRATIONS

Mr. William Thurston made the following assessment of the planning and budgeting effort:

> The effort to set goals and then to define programs accordingly has been invaluable for me, and also for all the managers involved in the process. It has given us a much better understanding of what is taking place in the company's operations and why each activity needs to be done, in terms of our objectives.
>
> Management faces some difficult problems in budgeting cost activities for GenRad. First, there are many competing needs for funds, many of which do not relate to each other in any simple way. Second, keeping track of all these activities has been difficult, especially when changes are made during the course of the year. Finally, we had no uniform criteria for evaluating the inclusion of different activities or for trimming them.
>
> What I like about ZBF is that it is a logical approach which gives high visibility to each of our programs. It helps us to keep track of what is going on, and it greatly facilitates making adjustments to our spending program.

[7] The number of increments was higher in the initial review.

This positive assessment of the recent planning and programming efforts was voiced by many other managers at GenRad. C. Landry had this to say:

One of the important benefits from the MBO and ZBF efforts has been to make it easier to discuss future activities with my subordinates. I can now show how each activity fits in the corporate scheme, and how it contributes specifically to one or more of Bill's [Thurston] corporate objectives. Tying the goals to the budget is also important. I have already had experience with MBO in my fourteen years with General Electric and my four years with Control Data. The problem there was that the objectives were not properly tied to the budget. More than once, you would be assigned a goal without access to the dollars needed to achieve the goal. Here, you are in a position to say "Either give me the money or get off my back."

One of the problems associated with the planning and budgeting efforts, all agreed, was the amount of management time devoted to generating the data. C. Landry estimated that "close to 70 percent of my 125 percent work load" over a four-month period had gone into setting goals, making plans and ranking cost activities. One of the divisional general managers was reported to have said, "In the seven weeks before Christmas, only three went into running the business." As another example of the time involved, Mr. Thurston estimated that the top management team spent ten days just in ranking the decision alternatives at the corporate level.

The heavy time commitment was attributed to the fact that "it was our first time through," and most managers agreed that much less time would be required in future cycles. The effort to include new projects and direct labor manufacturing activities in the ZBF as well as overhead items had added considerable burden. Some managers thought that GenRad had taken on too much by including these latter items. Mr. Stadler countered, "We thought it important to include all cost activities, not only those for overhead, so that we could reconcile the ZBF output with the corporate budget. It was a tough row to hoe, but I think we pulled it off." Another executive thought it important to recognize that the system "forced managers to spend a great deal of time on matters for which they should spend a great deal of time."[8]

A number of actual and potential problems were noted by various people who had been involved with the planning and budgeting effort. A financial executive feared that these efforts, which he saw as related to funding, could distract management attention from the budget. In 1976, the normal budgeting procedure had been delayed about three months so that it could follow the ZBF.

A concern raised by another manager was that people would soon find out how to play the system to their advantage. He surmised, "If some guy finds that listing more projects or identifying more alternative levels seems to get more funding, or vice versa, his approach will change accordingly. The motivation to use the system to personal advantage will be strong." One means to discourage this abuse as well as to ensure the quality of the cost estimates, according to a staff member who had had a responsibility for administering the ZBF, was to have a member of the Controllers

[8] In implementing the new planning and control system, management found it necessary or desirable to initiate numerous other undertakings. For example, in 1975, a physical inventory was taken for the first time and full absorption accounting was adopted. Also, job descriptions for managers were prepared.

Department review and check the cost figures in the original proposals. Under this procedure, the reviewer would either "sign off" if satisfied or note a dissent to the data.

This idea of checking the cost data was one of many ideas for improving the quality of the output and the effectiveness of the procedures followed. In addition to such corrective actions, management saw the need for additional elements in the scheme of planning and budgeting. Perhaps holding the highest priority was a need to devise means to keep track of and to control performance with respect to the many projects funded. Management incentive payments could then be tied to these results.

Top management also considered it important to extend the time horizon for planning. The 1975 Annual Operations Plan set forth the following objectives in this respect:

> Developing . . . a medium-term (3-5 years) Financial Planning Process . . . for use during 1976. . . .
>
> *   *   *   *   *
>
> Developing . . . a long-range (7-10 years) Planning System . . . for use during 1977 to develop long-range plans for the period through 1984 to 1987.[9]

[9] GR 11.3 and GR 11.4 as listed in Exhibit 3.

EXHIBIT 1
Partial organization chart, March 1976

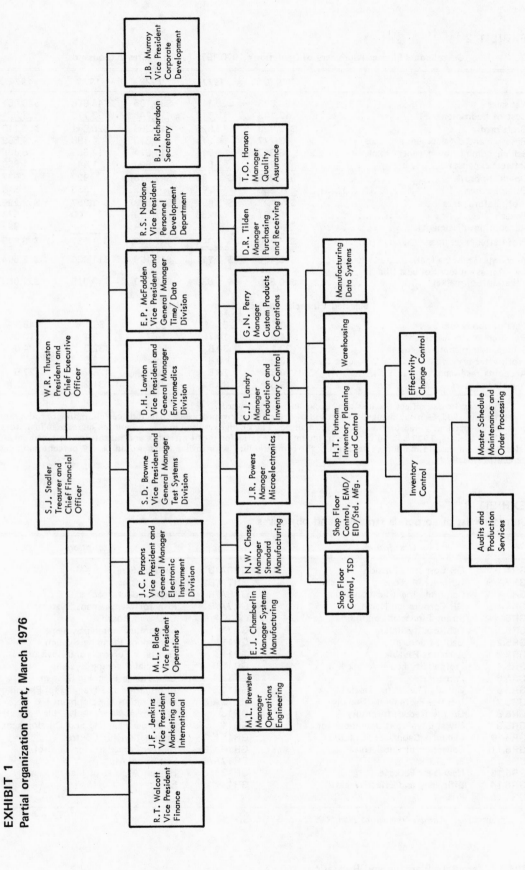

Source: Casewriter. Names disguised.

EXHIBIT 2

Consolidated Financial Summary of Operations, 1970-1974 (dollar figures in thousands)

	1970	1971	1972	1973	1974
Net sales	$26,096	$29,112	$33,105	$44,656	$48,961
Cost of goods sold	13,173	15,117	18,745	23,715	23,851
Gross profit	$12,923	$13,995	$14,360	$20,941	$25,110
Research and development expenses	3,777	4,271	4,870	4,195	4,899
Selling, administrative, general expense	8,642	8,914	11,614	14,383	16,665
Interest expense	732	611	694	1,441	1,869
Operating profit	$ (228)	$ 199	$ (2,818)	$ 922	$ 1,677
Other income	355	298	245	335	549
Profit before taxes	$ 127	$ 497	$ (2,573)	$ 1,257	$ 2,226
Taxes*	81	253	(270)	100	574
Accounting adjustment†	—	—	—	—	1,997
Profit after taxes (loss)	$ 46	$ 244	$ (2,303)	$ 1,157	$ 3,649
Accounts receivable (net)	$ 5,422	$ 7,711	$10,129	$11,936	$13,504
Inventories—at lower of cost (first-in, first-out) or market	$10,396	$ 9,833	$12,820	$13,918	$21,063

Selected Financial Ratios (percent of sales)

	1970	1971	1972	1973	1974
Cost of goods sold	50.5%	51.9%	56.6%	53.1%	48.7%
Research and development	14.5	14.7	14.7	9.4	10.0
Selling, administrative, general	33.1	30.6	35.1	32.2	34.0
Profit after tax	0.2	0.8	loss	2.6	†
Accounts receivable	20.8	26.5	30.6	26.7	27.6
Inventories	39.8	33.8	38.7	31.2	†

*The tax figures reflect tax loss carrybacks and carryforwards.

†During 1974, GenRad changed its method of determining inventory cost to include certain indirect production costs which previously had been expensed as incurred. The change resulted in a $3.85 million increase in inventory as of December 28, 1974 and an increase in income. The ratio for profit after tax and inventories as a percent of sales, based on the old method of accounting for comparability with earlier years, would be 3.4 percent and 35.2 percent, respectively.

EXHIBIT 3

Summary list of corporate strategies and objectives

Ref. Code	Description	Ref. Code	Description
GR1	GR Corporate Mission	GR6A/B	Physical Size
GR2A/B	Integrate Missions	GR7A/B	Grow Faster
GR3A/B	Corporate Identification	GR8A/B	New-Product Process
GR4A/B	GR Corporation Name	GR9A/B	Plan for Management System
GR5	Strong Financial Condition	GR10A/B	CEO and Board
GR5.1	Debt/Equity Ratio	GR11	Corporate Planning Systems
GR5.2	Debt Structure	GR11.1	Operations Planning System
GR5.3	Accounts Payable	GR11.2	Quarterly Forecasts and Revisions
GR5.4	Profitability above Average	GR11.3	Financial Planning System
GR5.5	Prime Rate	GR11.4	Long-Range Planning System
GR5.6	Outside Market for Stock	GR11.5	Information and Training for Planning
GR5.7	Increase Profitability Rapidly	GR12A/B	Organization Development
GR5.8	Greatly Reduce Inventory	GR13	Performance-Appraisal Skills
GR5.9	Divest Low-Profit Operations for Cash	GR14	Personnel Planning and Development
GR5.10	Minimize Capital Expenditures	GR15A/B	Information for Control
GR5.11	Collection of Receivables	GR16A/B	Review Procedure for Control
GR5.12	Sell Stock	GR17A/B	Self-Fulfillment
GR5.13	New Debt Package	GR18	Human Aspects of Management
GR5.14	Efficiency and Effectiveness	GR19	Esprit
GR5.15	Pricing		

Source: *GR Annual Operations Plan, 1975*, pp. 37-38.

EXHIBIT 4

Action item matrix prepared by W. Thurston (one of four work sheets)

General Radio

ACTION ITEM MATRIX   CORP-II

ASSIGNED TO: _____
RETURN TO: _____
DATE DUE _____
PREPARED BY: WRT
DATE: 5/75

UNIT MISSION STATEMENT

ORGANIZATIONAL UNIT	GR 5.6 Maintain Outside Market for Stock (Shorter than 5.12)	GR 5.7 Increase Profitability Rapidly (All to give annual & effort)	GR 5.8 Greatly Reduce Inventory	GR 5.9 Divest Low-Profit Operation: to Cash	GR 5.10 Minimize Capital Expenditure (All to avoid unless nec. to corp strategies)	GR 5.11 Collection of Receivables	GR 5.12 Sell Stock	GR 5.13 New Vent Purchase	GR 5.14 Efficiency & Effectiveness	GR 5.15 Pricing
CEO COO (WRT)		x		x Select	x				x all to suggest by goals, innovative alternatives in order PEE	
CFO Sr VP & Treas (SJS) Finance & Mgmt Info	x Develop plan Direct & coord implementation	x Develop plan Direct & coord implementation	x Prepare write-off pol. + Resp. reports	x Finan anal to identify candidate	x	x Policies, reports, Supervision	x Develop plan	x Develop plan toward GR 5.2	x	x Profitability info BJR
VP Corp Devel (JBM)	x	x		x manage divestment project	x				x	
Soc'ty & Legal (BJR)		x			x				x	
Personnel (RSN)		x			x				x	
Marketing & International (AFJ)	x	x	x Xero Do's Exhibit: Service		x	x GRD collect, customer satisfaction			x cont /business coord & implementation	
Operations (MLB)		x	x Raw matl's + in process parts		x				x	
EID (JCP)		x	x All EID		x	x EID collect			x	x price EID products
E&M (DHL)		x	x All E&M		x	x E&M collect			x	x price E&M products
TSD (SOB)		x	x All TSD		x	x SV collect			x	x price TSD products
T/D (EPM)		x	x All T/D		x	x T/D collect			x	x price T/D products

Note: Items circled relate to the statements of goals contained in Exhibits 5 and 6.

EXHIBIT 5
Excerpts from statement of goals prepared by S. Stadler

General Radio

PREPARED BY: S. J. Stadler

ORGANIZATION UNIT: Finance and MID

ON-GOING GOALS

PERCENTAGE OF TIME ALLOCATED TO ON-GOING GOALS _____ 70%

DATE PREPARED _____ September 15, 1975

MAJOR JOB FUNCTION	PERCENTAGE OF TOTAL TIME SPENT ON FUNCTION	PERFORMANCE MEASURE	COMMENTS
1. Assist the CEO in the development of goals, objectives and policies.	20%	The extent to which the assistance is requested and accepted.	In support of GR ALL
2. Provide the Board of Directors with financial reports, analysis and recommendations.	5%	The extent to which the material is understood and accepted.	In support of GR 11.2, 11.3, 11.4, 15, 16
3. Establish and approve policies, procedures and standards for ensuring the maintenance of adequate managerial and custodial accounting systems.	25%	The extent to which the systems enable managers to make timely decisions. The extent to which the systems yield timely data in compliance with the requirements of governmental authorities	In support of GR 11.2, 11.3, 11.4, 15, 16
4. Maintain favorable relations with the financial community to develop and maintain a viable capital structure.	20%	The extent to which capital can be obtained in the quantities required and at a cost that is competitive.	In support of GR 5.1, 5.2, 5.5, 5.6, 5.12, 5.13, 11.3
TOTAL _____ 70% (Should add up to figure in upper right corner)			

EXHIBIT 5 (continued)

 General Radio

PROBLEM SOLVING AND
INNOVATIVE GOALS

ORGANIZATION UNIT — GOAL	TYPE (PS or I)	PRELIMINARY COST/BENEFIT EVALUATION						DATE(S)	IMPLEMENTATION
		COST			BENEFIT				
		MAJOR	MODER-ATE	MINOR	MAJOR	MODER-ATE	MINOR		
3. Implement uniform manufacturing cost systems at all manufacturing units to facilitate individual product cost reports of actual and standard manufacturing costs.	PS		X		X			6/76 GRM 12/76 GRW	In support of GR 5.4, 5.7, 5.8, 5.9, 5.14, 5.15, 8
4. Issue guidelines for the treatment of obsolete or excess inventories of parts, assemblies and finished products.	PS			X		X		12/75	In support of GR 5.8
6. Issue formulae for use by product managers, their product design staff, and manufacturing managers in make-buy decisions.	PS			X	X			12/75	In support of GR 5.4, 5.7, 5.8, 8
9. Design and implement uniform accounting systems at all corporate units to assign assets, particularly the various categories of inventory, to corporate unit managers.	I		X		X			12/76	In support of GR 5.1, 5.4, 5.8, 5.9, 5.11, 11, 11.3, 11.4, 15
10. With reference to #9, above, develop guidelines and mechanisms that will assign responsibility to corporate unit managers for the maintenance of appropriate asset levels and will measure their performance.	I		X		X			12/76	In support of same corporate objectives as #9, above.

OPERATIONS CORPORATE UNIT, Objective No. 2

Title: Inventory Reduction   Supports: G.R. Corporate Objective No. 5.8

Inventory turn ratios at GR/M are at best one half of acceptable ratios in comparable operations. Inventories represent our most ineffectively used asset. This problem is really a significant opportunity to assist in reaching a satisfactory financial condition (balance sheet) and to improve profitability by reducing interest expense.

This Operations objective is assigned to improve the levels of "unfinished inventory" consisting of raw materials, parts, and work-in-process. Two major activities are required to accomplish this. First, improvement in the systems and methods used to control inventory at the detail item level and second, improvement in the process of regulating output from manufacturing activities to support Marketing requirements.

>—————

Operations Action Item No. 2.1: Master Schedule Control

Careful examination and monitoring at the top level is required due to extensive impact on inventory levels and labor and material activities. Production and Inventory Control is primarily responsible for maintenance of the Master Schedule and subsequent explosions of requirements placed on labor and material allocations. Close coordination with Marketing is required to assure optimum service levels consistent with minimum inventory levels.

Specific Notes:

Production, Inventory Control: Continue programs to maintain Master Schedule to drive Manufacturing activities in close coordination with Marketing Administration on Net Requirements Generator. Work with GRAPICS, Accounting, and M/S to absorb independent demands and insert directly in Master Schedule and work order system.

>—————

Operations Action Item No. 2.2: New Product Introduction Schedule

Specific Notes:

Production, Inventory Control: Close coordination with Project Management and Operations Engineering for smooth phase-in with minimum inventories.

>—————

Operations Action Item No. 2.3: Obsolescence Program

Specific Notes:

Production, Inventory Control: Identify low-volume products and options for analysis and action. Identify items for excessively long supply and recommend action.

Specific Goals:

Review all items with over three years' usage based on 1975 usage rate and projected demands.

>—————

Operations Action Item No. 2.4: Cycle Time Reduction

Specific Notes:

Production, Inventory Control: Optimize scheduling activities to reduce queue times at all stations. Recommend stocking of long lead items.

>—————

Operations Action Item No. 2.5: GRAPICS

The largest impact from GRAPICS is expected to be in inventory control and reduction because of improved systems capability and management visibility. GRAPICS will identify quantities and time phased requirements for items at all levels with high accuracy based on minimum cost algorithms.

Source: 28 page document dated September 24, 1975.   >————— indicates a change in page.

EXHIBIT 7
Decision package for inventory control

GR General Radio

| 5 | 1 | 1 | | | | |

Page 1 of 2

(1) DECISION UNIT NAME:
Inventory Planning & Control (XXX)

(2) CORPORATE UNIT: Operations

(3) LEVEL A ORGANIZATION UNIT:
Production & Inventory Control

(4) LEVEL B ORGANIZATION UNIT (S):
Inventory Planning & Control (XXX)

(5) LEVEL C ORGANIZATION UNIT (S):
Inventory Control (131, 137, 152)

(6) PREPARED BY:
H. T. Putnam

(7) DATE: 11-12-75

(9) DESCRIBE CURRENT SERVICES PROVIDED, RESOURCES USED, DIRECT CLIENTS OF SERVICE, AND HOW THE DECISION UNIT OPERATES: Four (4) managers and eleven (11) clerks develop and maintain the total Mfg Plan and all other independent demands for material.

Material Control functions include FISR interface, Misc. Use Planning & Control, shop supply ordering & purchasing interface.
Inventory Control functions include Job & Stock status maintenance, auditing and annual physical inventory, shop paper work, preparation and Master Schedule maintenance.

(10) DESCRIBE DESIRED MEANS OF ACCOMPLISHING THIS DECISION UNIT'S GOALS:
Inventory Planning & Control is organized to operate the Manufacturing Master Schedule through FISR meetings with Marketing Division representatives and then operate the ordering and inventory control systems necessary to execute the Master Schedule.

(11) LIST DISCARDED ALTERNATIVE MEANS OF ACCOMPLISHING THIS DECISION UNIT'S GOALS AND REASONS FOR DISCARDING ALTERNATIVES:
This 'B' levels work elements are largely clerical in nature due to the current Mfg Systems which it uses. Changes to these systems would make possible some people reduction however with GRAPICS implementation on the near horizon. This alternative was discarded.

(12) SUMMARY OF DECISION PACKAGE INCREMENTS	1975 PROJECTED		15		225			CAPITAL EXPENSES CUM. 1976	INVENT. COM. CUM. 1976
		POSITIONS		OPERATING EXPENSES					
		1976 INCR	1976 CUM	1976 INCR.	1976 CUM.	%CUM 76/75			
1 of 8 Minimum Level (2 Mgrs. - 9 Clerks)		11	11	182	182	.81			
2 of 8 Material Slip Review Clerk		1	12	10	192	.85			
3 of 8 Cycle Count & Inventory Transaction Analysis		2	14	24	216	.96			
* 4 of 8 Mfg Emergency Keypunch Capability		1	15	13	229	1.02			
* 5 of 8 Effectivity Change Control (1 Mgr. 1 anal., 3 clerks)		3	18	49	278	1.24			
6 of 8 Material Planners		2	20	36	314	1.40			
7 of 8 Excess & Obsolete Inv. Analyst		1	21	16	330	1.47			
* 8 of 8 Reports Distribution Clerk		1	22	9.4	339	1.51			

*Increments not included in the exhibit.

EXHIBIT 7 (continued)

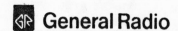
General Radio

ZERO-BASE BUDGETING OVERHEAD
MINIMUM LEVEL OF EFFORT   INCREMENTAL ANALYSIS

$(000)

(1) DECISION UNIT NAME: Inventory Planning & Control (XXX)	(13) RESOURCES REQUIRED	1974 ACT	1975 BUDG	1975 PROJ.	1976 PROP.
	POSITIONS - THIS INCREMENT				11
(14) DESCRIBE OPERATIONS PERFORMED AND SERVICES PROVIDED:	POSITIONS - CUMULATIVE	29	16	15	11
	OPERATING EXPENSE - THIS INCREMENT				182
Two (2) Managers & nine (9) clerks would provide only those services that would keep the material flowing to the Master Schedule demands.	OPERATING EXPENSE - CUMULATIVE	316	215	225	182
	OPERATING EXPENSE - % PRIOR YEAR		.68	.71	.81
(Ed. note: The reduction of personnel from 29 to 16 reflected a transfer of computer programmers to another department.)	CAPITAL EXPENSE - THIS INCREMENT				-
	CAPITAL EXPENSE- CUMULATIVE				
	INVENTORY COMMITMENT- THIS INCREMENT				-
	INVENTORY COMMITMENT- CUMULATIVE	-	-	-	-

(15) DESCRIBE CHANGES FROM CURRENT OPERATIONS:
1) Material Slip Reviews for unallocated material availability would be discontinued.
2) P56 Ordering Analysis would stop.
3) IP & C Operating procedures would not be documented.
4) Measurement reporting and variance analysis would be done on a time available basis.

(16) DESCRIBE BENEFITS OF APPROVING THIS INCREMENT:
Reduction of one (1) Manager and one (1) clerk would save the corporation $24.K in 1976.

(17) OPERATING EXPENSES % 76/75 FOR MINIMUM LEVEL OF EFFORT____.82_____
REASONS WHY LOWER LEVEL OF EFFORT WAS NOT CHOSEN:
Any further decrease in manning would make it impossible to maintain the flow of material to the Master Schedule and other independent demand requestors.

(18) WORKLOAD/PERFORMANCE MEASUREMENTS:	1974 ACT.	1975 PROJ	1976 THIS INCR.	1976 CUM.	% CUM. OF 1975
Increase of parts shorts at kit issue & resultant schedule adherence reduction		TI from 2 to 6 wks late			
Increase in WIP by putting the PTI to GTI safe time back in the Master Schedule		600K WIP increase			

EXHIBIT 7 (continued)

◈ General Radio

ZERO-BASE BUDGETING OVERHEAD
ADDITIONAL LEVEL OF EFFORT INCREMENTAL ANALYSIS

$(000)

(1) DECISION UNIT NAME: Inventory Planning and Control	(13) RESOURCES REQUIRED	1974 ACT	1975 BUDG	1975 PROJ.	1976 PROP.
	POSITIONS - THIS INCREMENT				1
(14) DESCRIBE OPERATIONS PERFORMED AND SERVICES PROVIDED: One (1) clerk added to perform Material Slip Review and P56 ordering analysis.	POSITIONS -- CUMULATIVE	29	16	15	12
	OPERATING EXPENSE - THIS INCREMENT				10
	OPERATING EXPENSE - CUMULATIVE	316	215	225	194
	OPERATING EXPENSE - % PRIOR YEAR		.68	.71	.86
	CAPITAL EXPENSE - THIS INCREMENT				-
	CAPITAL EXPENSE- CUMULATIVE				-
	INVENTORY COMMITMENT - THIS INCREMENT				-
	INVENTORY COMMITMENT - CUMULATIVE	-	-	-	-

(15) DESCRIBE CHANGES FROM CURRENT OPERATIONS:

Reduction of one (1) manager from current staff would stop all efforts to document IP & C procedures and inventory transaction audits and analyses would be curtailed.

(16) DESCRIBE BENEFITS OF APPROVING THIS INCREMENT:

The material slip reviews would be continued to assure use of material for its planned use. The P56 ordering analysis would be continued to assure proper qty ordering.

(19) IMPACT OF NOT FUNDING THIS INCREMENT:

Problem inventory transactions would not be analyzed to resolve the problem source and thus guarantee accurate inventory records and corresponding ordering actions appropriate.

(18) WORKLOAD/PERFORMANCE MEASUREMENTS:	1974 ACT.	1975 PROJ.	1976 THIS INCR.	1976 CUM.	% CUM. OF 1975
Maintain part shorts at current level and no increase in WIP inventory			TI no more than 2 wks late		

EXHIBIT 7 (continued)

⟨GR⟩ General Radio

ZERO-BASE BUDGETING OVERHEAD
ADDITIONAL LEVEL OF EFFORT   INCREMENTAL ANALYSIS

Increment __3__ of __8__

$(000)

(1) DECISION UNIT NAME:	(13) RESOURCES REQUIRED	1974 ACT	1975 BUDG	1975 PROJ.	1976 PROP.
Inventory Planning and Control	POSITIONS - THIS INCREMENT				2
(14) DESCRIBE OPERATIONS PERFORMED AND SERVICES PROVIDED:	POSITIONS -- CUMULATIVE	29	16	15	14
	OPERATING EXPENSE - THIS INCREMENT				24
Add one (1) manager and one (1) cycle count clerical analyst to perform all cycle count variance analyses and record adjustments, all inventory transaction problem analyses and IP & C procedures preparation.	OPERATING EXPENSE - CUMULATIVE	316	215	225	218
	OPERATING EXPENSE - % PRIOR YEAR		.68	.71	.97
	CAPITAL EXPENSE - THIS INCREMENT				-
	CAPITAL EXPENSE- CUMULATIVE				-
	INVENTORY COMMITMENT - THIS INCREMENT				-
	INVENTORY COMMITMENT - CUMULATIVE	-	-	-	-

(15) DESCRIBE CHANGES FROM CURRENT OPERATIONS:

Changes current operation over from annual physical inventory to weekly cycle count variance analysis and adjustments.

See SFC Incr. 4 of 6 & whse Incr. 3 of 5

(16) DESCRIBE BENEFITS OF APPROVING THIS INCREMENT:

There will be an overall increase in the accuracy of inventory records and resultant order actions. The amount of erroneous inventory planning will be reduced by timely correction of the source of the problems.

(19) IMPACT OF NOT FUNDING THIS INCREMENT:

1) Continued need for annual physical inventory.
2) High level of inventory record inaccuracies.
3) Continued need for high expediting costs and safety stock levels higher than required.

(18) WORKLOAD/PERFORMANCE MEASUREMENTS:	1974 ACT.	1975 PROJ.	1976 THIS INCR.	1976 CUM.	% CUM. OF 1975
Eliminate the requirement for a full annual stores inventory			6/76		
Reduce record inaccuracies as a % of total inventory $	2%	2%	1%		
Decision to reduce or eliminate current safety stocks	50K	200K	Range 0-100K		

EXHIBIT 7 (continued)

General Radio

ZERO-BASE BUDGETING OVERHEAD
ADDITIONAL LEVEL OF EFFORT INCREMENTAL ANALYSIS

$(000)

(1) DECISION UNIT NAME:	(13) RESOURCES REQUIRED	1974 ACT	1975 BUDG.	1975 PROJ.	1976 PROP.
Inventory Planning and Control	POSITIONS - THIS INCREMENT				2
(14) DESCRIBE OPERATIONS PERFORMED AND SERVICES PROVIDED:	POSITIONS - CUMULATIVE	29	16	15	20
Add two (2) material planners to resolve FISR generated master schedule change request problems and establish commitment dates for instrument/systems deliveries to plan and order subassemblies impacted by FISR changes and assist SFC and Purchasing with demand problems and errors.	OPERATING EXPENSE - THIS INCREMENT				36
	OPERATING EXPENSE - CUMULATIVE	316	215	225	316
	OPERATING EXPENSE - % PRIOR YEAR		.68	.71	1.40
	CAPITAL EXPENSE - THIS INCREMENT				-
	CAPITAL EXPENSE - CUMULATIVE				-
	INVENTORY COMMITMENT - THIS INCREMENT				-
	INVENTORY COMMITMENT - CUMULATIVE	-	-	-	-

(15) DESCRIBE CHANGES FROM CURRENT OPERATIONS:

Transfer work tasks currently performed by the manager Inventory Planning and Control plus begin the planning subassemblies impacted by FISR revisions.

(16) DESCRIBE BENEFITS OF APPROVING THIS INCREMENT:

Will relieve the Manager IP & C of FISR generated analytical work tasks and allow him to spend more of his time on inventory measurement and reduction and GRAPICS specification.

(19) IMPACT OF NOT FUNDING THIS INCREMENT:

Manager of IP & C will continue excessive involvement in the FISR created detail analyses and will not be able to spend adequate time in inventory reduction and GRAPICS specifications.

(18) WORKLOAD/PERFORMANCE MEASUREMENTS:	1974 ACT.	1975 PROJ.	1976 THIS INCR.	1976 CUM.	% CUM. OF 1975
Improve response to marketing change requests within a FISR cycle		%	100%		
Maintain current level of Master Schedule and inventory reduction			X		
Increased Manager attention to MCS/MRP GRAPICS specification and implementation			X		

EXHIBIT 7 (concluded)

◈ General Radio

ZERO-BASE BUDGETING OVERHEAD
ADDITIONAL LEVEL OF EFFORT — INCREMENTAL ANALYSIS

S(000)

(1) DECISION UNIT NAME: Inventory Planning and Control	(13) RESOURCES REQUIRED	1974 ACT.	1975 BUDG.	1975 PROJ.	1976 PROP.
	POSITIONS - THIS INCREMENT				1
(14) DESCRIBE OPERATIONS PERFORMED AND SERVICES PROVIDED:	POSITIONS -- CUMULATIVE	29	16	15	21
	OPERATING EXPENSE - THIS INCREMENT				16
Add one (1) analyst to perform excess and obsolete inventory analyses for inventory disposal and cycle time analyses to isolate potential areas for improvements.	OPERATING EXPENSE - CUMULATIVE	316	215	225	332
	OPERATING EXPENSE - % PRIOR YEAR		.68	.71	1.48
	CAPITAL EXPENSE - THIS INCREMENT				-
	CAPITAL EXPENSE - CUMULATIVE				-
	INVENTORY COMMITMENT - THIS INCREMENT				-
	INVENTORY COMMITMENT - CUMULATIVE	-	-	-	-

(15) DESCRIBE CHANGES FROM CURRENT OPERATIONS:

Begin reviewing obsoleted inventories prior to the final removal from item master and product structures. Review and dispose of excess years supply of parts/assemblies in excess of corporate guidelines. Develope procedures and implement an"Obsolete Instrument Spares Provision Program" to support products in their "Service Support Phase".

(16) DESCRIBE BENEFITS OF APPROVING THIS INCREMENT:

1. Reduction of excess and obsolete inventory by $200K to $300K during 1976.
2. Identification areas where total product cycle times can be reduced.

(19) IMPACT OF NOT FUNDING THIS INCREMENT:

1. Excess and obsolete inventories will not be reduced to the level possible with this increment.
2. Cycle Time analyses will receive little or no attention.

(18) WORKLOAD/PERFORMANCE MEASUREMENTS:	1974 ACT.	1975 PROJ.	1976 THIS INCR.	1976 CUM.	% CUM. OF 1975
Reduce the level of Raw & Parts inventory with over (5) years supply	580K	520K	320K		
Reduce levels of other inventories		Measure to be established			

EXHIBIT 8
Decision package ranking at the level of Production and Inventory Control

General Radio

DECISION PACKAGE RANKING

Note: Items 2, 7, 8, 13, and 14 correspond to the first five alternatives in Exhibit 11.

—29—   176-227

(1) RANK	(2) DECISION PACKAGES — DECISION UNIT NAME	INCREMENT	(3) 1976 PROPOSED POS.	OP. EXP.	(4) 1976 CUMULATIVE POS.	OP. EXP.	(5) 1976 CAP EXPENSE INCR.	CUMUL.	(6) 1976 INV COMMITMENT INCR.	CUMUL. ($000)
1	P&C Admin – Minimum	3,1	4	139 / 299.	4	139 / 299.	—	—	—	—
2	IP&C – Minimum	3,1	11	182 / 484.	15	321 / 383.	—	—	—	—
3	SFC – Minimum	3,1	28	378 / 374.	43	699 / 877.				
4	Warehouse	3,1	14	195 / 262.	57	894 / 1,009.				
5	Mfg. Data Systems	3,1	7	125.	64	1019 / 1,144.				
6	P&C Admin – Mgr. SFC Sys	3,1	1	20.	65	1039 / 1,164.				
7	IP&C – Matl Slip Review	3,1	1	10.	66	1049 / 1,174.				
8	IP&C – Cycle Count Analysis	3,1	2	24.	68	1073 / 1,198.				
9	SFC – Cycle Counting	3,1	1	12.	69	1085 / 1,210.				
10	Warehouse – Cycle Counting	3,1	2	21.	71	1106 / 1,231.				
11	SFC – Systems Expeditor	3,1	1	11.	72	1117 / 1,242.				
12	SFC – Std Mfg. Expeditor	3,1	1	12.	73	1129 / 1,254.				
13	IP&C – Material Planners	3,1	2	36.	75	1165 / 1,290.				
14	IP&C – Effect. Change Control	3,1	3	49.	78	1214 / 1,339.				
15	Warehouse – Summer OT	3,1			71	1059 / 1,229.				

PRIOR YEAR'S RECAP

ORGANIZATIONAL UNITS BEING RANKED: Production & Inventory Control

PREPARED BY: C. J. Landry

DATE: 11/3/75

PAGE 1 of 2

EXHIBIT 9
Selected items from the decision package ranking statement for the Operations Corporate Unit

General Radio

DECISION PACKAGE RANKING ($.000)

CORP UNIT	DEPT	INC	DEC PKG #	RANK	INCREMENT DESCRIPTION	Positions INC	Positions CUM	Op Exp INC	Op Exp CUM	Cap Exp INC	Cap Exp CUM	Inv Level INC	Inv Level CUM	Other: Positions CUM (description)
					(Items ranked 1 through 23 listed)									
3/1			01	024	WAREHOUSE	14	249	195	4776	—	83	—	1057	(14 STOCK PEOPLE)
3/1	*		01	025	INV. PLAN + CONT	11	260	182	4958	—	83	—	1051	(11 CLERICAL)
3/1			01	044	PT + 1C ADMIN	4	454	139	8455	—	133	—	1541	(MGRS)
3/1	*		02	057	INV. PLAN + CONT	1	498	10	9673	—	173	—	1548	(MAT. SLIP REVIEW)
3/1		2	02	079	MICRO-ELECT. MFG	—	542	2	10279	25	298	(2)	1546	(LASER CUTTING)
3/1	*		03	088	INV. PLAN + CONT	2	554	24	10472	—	300	-1	1546	(CYCLE COUNT - CONC)
3/1			02	109	ENG. MACH SHOP-BOLT	1	584	18	11016	—	336	—	1546	(TOOL + DIE MAKER) current level
3/1			02	116	QUALITY ENGRS	2	604	45	11640	—	601	—	1546	(1 INCOMING, 1 FLOOR ENGR)
3/1	*		06	117	INV. PLAN + CONT	2	606	36 (25K)	11676	—	601	—	1546	(2 PLANNERS, MASTER SKED)
3/1	*		05	118	INV PLAN + CONT	3	609	45	11725	—	601	—	1546	(CHANGE CONTROL)
3/1	*		07	119	INV PLAN + CONT	1	610	6	11761	—	601	—	1546	(EXCESS + OBSOL. INV)
3/1			04	120	DRAFTING	2	612	37	11778	—	601	—	1546	(CHECKERS)
3/1	*		08	150	INV. PLAN + CONT	1	644	9	12308	—	724	—	1546	(REPORTS CLERK)
3/1			04	152	IN-PROC + FINAL INSP	1	646	25 (RMA)	12548	30	754	—	1546	
					PRIOR YEAR'S RECAP E.O.Y.		558		11048					7 · 149

ORGANIZATIONAL UNITS BEING RANKED: **OPERATIONS CORPORATE UNIT**

M&D INTERNAL PROJECTS

PREPARED BY: **M. BLAKE** DATE: 11-19-75 PAGE ___ OF 22

*Note: The original document included 152 items in consecutive order of rank. Items marked with an asterisk relate to the decision package contained in Exhibit 11.

EXHIBIT 10
Excerpts from the decision package ranking computer printout for GenRad, Inc.

DECISION UNIT ANALYSIS BY RANK

IN CR	RNK	DESCRIPTION	CORPORATE UNIT				OTHER RESOURCE UNITS			
			POS	OPR EXP	CAP EXP	INV	POS	OPR EXP	CAP EXP	INV
13	188 OPR—	MATERIAL ENGRG—MLE	1.0	61.0	0.0	0.0	0.0	0.0	0.0	0.0
22	189 OPR—	OPERATIONS MGMT	1.0	30.0	0.0	0.0	0.0	0.0	0.0	0.0
*29	190 OPR—	INV PLAN + CONT	1.0	10.0	0.0	0.0	0.0	0.0	0.0	0.0
04	191 OPR—	CONCORD BUILDING	1.0	9.0	0.0	0.0	0.0	0.0	0.0	0.0
05	192 OPR—	CONCORD BLDG	2.0	34.0	0.0	0.0	0.0	0.0	0.0	0.0
										PAGE 4
23	218 OPR—	MFG DOCUMENT	2.0	20.0	0.0	0.0	0.0	0.0	0.0	0.0
23	219 OPR—	MATERIAL ENGRG	1.0	26.0	0.0	0.0	0.0	0.0	0.0	0.0
*39	220 OPR—	INV PLAN + CONT	2.0	24.0	0.0	0.0	0.0	0.0	0.0	0.0
68	221 OPR—	WAREHOUSE	2.0	21.0	0.0	0.0	0.0	0.0	0.0	0.0
47	222 OPR—	SHOP FLOOR CONT	1.0	7.0	0.0	0.0	0.0	0.0	0.0	0.0
										PAGE 5
24	322 TSD—	CUSTOMER SERVICES	1.0	20.6	0.0	0.0	0.0	0.0	0.0	0.0
12	323 OPR—	GRAPICS PROJECT	12.5	366.5	16.0	0.0	6.0	–163.0	0.0	0.0
*59	324 OPR—	INV PLAN + CONT — CHANGE	3.0	40.0	0.0	0.0	0.0	0.0	0.0	0.0
45	325 ADM—	MID OPR GRAPHICS HARDWAR	0.0	25.0	0.0	0.0	0.0	0.0	0.0	0.0
33	326 OPR—	CPO ADMIN	1.0	22.0	0.0	0.0	0.0	0.0	0.0	0.0
										PAGE 6

*Items relate to alternatives 2, 3, and 5 in the decision package contained in Exhibit 11. The ranking on this printout was based on an earlier version of the decision package which proposed nine alternatives instead of eight and had slightly different cost data.

Index